PREGNANCY, CHILDREN, and the VEGAN DIET

by MICHAEL KLAPER, M.D.

Printed
on
Recycled Paper

DEDICATION

For parents and children everywhere
Whose food choices will determine their destiny
And that of our life-giving planet

NOTICE TO READERS

The information in this book is intended to serve as a guideline to help plan an adequate nutritional program free of meat, dairy, and other animal products, for adults, children, and pregnant women, in good health. The nutritional values cited are accepted averages derived for the general population from accredited nutritional sources. Should any physical condition exist requiring medical treatment or special consideration, nutritional advice from the appropriate professional (M.D., R.D., etc.) should be sought. Do not change medications without consulting the proper health professional.

© Copyright 1987

Reprint: September 1991

ISBN 0-9614248-2-6

Gentle World, Inc.

P.O. Box U
Paia, Maui, HI 96779

Vegan mother and daughter, MARCIA PEARSON and TAHIRA

TABLE OF CONTENTS

Chapter 4
THE VEGAN DIET FOR CHILDREN

Vegan lad KYLE CHIDESTER at 3 years of age.

FOREWORD FOR HEALTH PROFESSIONALS

Among those physicians, dietitians, and others with a professional interest in nutrition and health, there may be some who are not familiar with pure vegetarian (vegan) nutrition. Some may question the suitability of such a dietary approach for pregnant women and growing children. **PREGNANCY, CHILDREN, and THE VEGAN DIET** presents the rationale for animal-free nutrition, and a guide to its proper application.

The increasing importance of the role of vegetarian nutrition in modern life makes this book of special value to the health practitioner and diet counselor.

We now live in a world of Salmonella-tainted chickens, Listeria-covered cheese, and beefburgers laced with estrogenic hormones and residues of potent antibiotics. There are **very good reasons** why parents would want to raise their son or daughter without fatty and contaminated meat and dairy products pouring through the child's bloodstream each day.

The practice of pure vegetarian nutrition is an established and growing reality. People around the planet are thriving on a vegan-style diet, having healthy babies and raising children, as they have done throughout history. As vegetarians are encountered in clinical practice, a knowledge of the principles of animal-free nutrition is helpful in understanding their clients' nutritional strategies, and in planning health-promoting diet choices.

Many parents and parents-to-be, concerned about the rising incidence of grave health threats linked to diet, like birth defects, childhood leukemia, and cardiovascular disease, are seeking more wholesome food alternatives for their families. Others do not want to contribute to the violence inherent in meat production, such as that inflicted upon animals during factory farming, or at the slaughterhouse. Still others hope to heal our planet's troubled ecosystem, with its vanishing rain forests and dwindling water supplies, by utilizing the vegan nutritional approach. Thus, for many reasons, the awareness of the advantages of a flesh-free diet is rapidly increasing, as are the numbers of those who are benefiting from its practice.

The rationale for pure vegetarian nutrition is supported by sound scientific principles. The clinician and nutritionist should feel comfortable with the fact that it is physiologically and biochemically possible (and even easy) for a woman to properly nourish herself, carry a successful full-term pregnancy, and raise a healthy child, on a diet **free** of animal products.

The body of Homo sapiens has no nutritional requirement for the flesh of animals, for the eggs of chickens, or for the milk of cows. A brief review of biochemical principles will confirm that the human body can derive all essential nutrients from a vegetarian diet.

Human health and growth requires sufficient supplies of the following essential nutrients:

1. **Carbohydrates** ⎱
2. **Fats** ⎰ **Energy (calories)**
3. **Protein**
4. **Vitamins**
5. **Minerals**
6. **Water**

Considering each nutrient individually, the body's **energy** needs are met by 2-carbon acetate groups that feed the Krebs citric acid cycle. The energy is stored as adenosine triphosphate (ATP). The (2-carbon) "cell fuel" for this process abounds in the **carbohydrates** and **fats** found in the starches, sugars, and oils in grains, potatoes, fruits, nuts, and seeds. A well-planned vegan diet amply supplies adequate calories.

The two essential **fatty acids**, linoleic acid and linolenic acid, needed for normal **fat** metabolism, are found abundantly in nuts, seeds, grains, and cooking oils.

All the essential **amino acids** required for human **protein** metabolism are contained in the high-quality proteins in grains, legumes, seeds, nuts, and green vegetables - and without undue concern for "protein combining."

All essential **vitamins** and **minerals** are found in green and yellow vegetables and fruits. In cases such as pregnancy or during an illness, when selected vitamin and mineral supplementation (B-12, calcium, etc.) may be deemed necessary, these can also be supplied through non-animal sources.

Thus, three balanced vegan meals daily, based upon grains, legumes, vegetables, fruits, nuts and seeds, will provide ample amounts of all the above nutrients for adults (pregnant or not) and growing children. Women eating in a vegan style have been shown to have normal pregnancies (with less preeclampsia[56a]), and their children grow to be full-size adults, largely free of the degenerative diseases that plague their meat-eating peers [31,33].

More and more people are seeking information on a plant-based diet, as it offers the promise of better health, and a safer, more plentiful world for themselves and their children.* **PREGNANCY, CHILDREN, and THE VEGAN DIET** is offered to professionals and parents to help in this important educational process.

Michael Klaper, M.D.
Eustis, Florida
1988

*See "An Ancient Vision for a Brighter Future."

AN IMPORTANT QUESTION

The young mother or mother-to-be, moving towards vegetarianism, must feel confident about an important question: **can one create and sustain a healthy pregnancy, and raise strong, full-size, healthy children, on a diet free of meat and dairy products?** She is likely to hear various opinions from friends, family members, and the professional community.

This question deserves careful consideration. There are responsible physicians and nutritionists who express reservations about pure vegetarian nutrition, especially during pregnancy and childraising. Medical journals do contain scattered reports of unusual cases where nutritionally unaware parents have inflicted unbalanced diets upon their children[29]. The resulting cases of vitamin deficiency were significant, though fortunately, most problems disappeared promptly and completely when the deficient vitamin was supplied through food and/or supplements[30].

Instances of severe nutritional imbalance should not occur on a properly planned, plant-based diet. The human body runs extremely efficiently on foods derived exclusively from plant sources, as basic textbooks in biochemistry or physiology will confirm[25]. Creating a balanced, fully nutritious vegan diet is not difficult; however, a woman or couple choosing vegan nutrition for themselves and for their children must take seriously their responsibility for learning the fundamentals of what their bodies require, and what foods will meet those requirements.

One must assure, especially during pregnancy and childrearing, that nutrients like protein, calories, and necessary vitamins and minerals, are abundant in the diet. **PREGNANCY, CHILDREN, and the VEGAN DIET** makes clear which foods contain these nutrients, and provides the guidelines to vegan food selection to help the reader feel nutritionally confident at mealtime. Its pages will also introduce the basic ingredients and meal ideas from the delicious world of vegan cuisine, adapted for the special needs of pregnant women and growing children.

In answer to the "important question" - yes, vegan nutrition works. In their landmark studies, Drs. Frey Ellis[31] and T.A.B. Sanders[32] documented that vegan mothers have successful pregnancies[24a-c,33], and raise healthy, full-size vegan children[24d-f,34]. A flesh-free diet has produced health and strength in people around the world throughout history[35]. It can do the same for you and your family.

Vegan from birth, ROSE PEDEN, at 8 months.

Chapter 1

PERSPECTIVES ON NUTRITION

In recent years, the importance of nutrition has evolved greatly in the minds of many nutritionists, scientists, and physicians. It is clear that within minutes of eating anything, elements of that food are flowing through every cell in the body, including the brain, muscles, glands, and skin. As the components of your last meal flow through your bloodstream, they create changes in the function of every organ and in the balance of every body system. The muscle tension in the walls of arteries, the levels of vital hormones, the mineral regulation in the kidneys, and thousands of other subtle, but important balances, are all affected by every food you eat.

These proteins and other substances then actually **become** your tissues, become YOU. **If you are a pregnant woman, these foods and any possible chemical contaminants they contain, become your baby**. Your growing child truly is composed of all the food he or she has eaten in the past, and will become an adult made of the foods she or he will eat from now on.

Current medical journals, as well as the mass media, are filled with reports of the suffering from illnesses spawned by improper diet. The **concentrated animal fats and proteins** found in **meat, eggs, and dairy products**, (as well as **refined sugars**), are the major villains in most Americans' poor food habits[1].

In addition, the **contaminating chemicals**[2], **bacteria**[3], **cancer viruses**[4], and **saturated fats**[5] in the meat/poultry/dairy-based American diet, pose a special hazard for pregnant women and growing children.

1. **Meat and poultry** are prone to harbor treacherous, antibiotic-resistant, **Camplyobacter and Salmonella bacteria**, whose diarrheal intestinal infections can be devastating during pregnancy[6] and fatal to children[7].

2. **Dairy products** often have contaminants, like **antibiotic residues** in milk and Listeria **bacteria** in cheese, infamous for causing babies to be born with infected nervous systems (meningitis)[8].

3. **Fish** frequently live in contaminated lakes, rivers, and bays. Thus, their flesh is often tainted with measurable doses of cancer and mutation-producing substances. **Hydrocarbon pesticides**[11a] (PCB's, dioxin, etc.) can produce severe cell mutations, as can **radioactivity** from nuclear wastes[8b]. These toxins, as well as **heavy metals**[8c], like mercury and lead[8d], which can produce kidney damage[9] in mothers, and cause babies to be born blind[10], and mentally retarded[11], are all being found more frequently in fish flesh in recent years. These substances contaminate the bodies of mothers and fetus[11b] and the pesticides appear in significant amounts in the mother's breastmilk.

The oil in fish has been associated with decreased blood-clotting ability, a potentially dangerous problem at birthing time[11c]. Women who consume large amounts of oily fish have a greater risk of the pregnancy being prolonged past term. This delay allows the baby to become abnormally large, and frequently causes birth complications like bleeding and difficult labors, more cesarean sections, and more maternal deaths[11d].

4. **Shellfish**, like clams, oysters, shrimp, and scallops, can contain **hepatitis virus**, that causes a debilitating, and sometimes deadly, liver infection in adults and children[12].

5. **Meat**[13], **fish**[14], and **dairy products**[15], commonly contain traces of **hydrocarbon chemicals** like heptachlor, dieldrin, hexachlorobenzene, and PCB's and PBB's (polybrominated biphenyls). These toxic residues from industrial pollution and agricultural spraying of herbicides and pesticides accumulate in the flesh and milk of animals who eat sprayed feed grains and drink polluted water. Consequently, they appear in significant amounts in flesh foods and milk products[16,17].

6. **Beef and chicken** flesh contain measurable amounts of female hormones (estrogens and stilbesterol) fed to the animal to increase weight, fat content, or egg production. These powerful sex hormones, potent in tiny amounts (parts per **trillion**) appear in active form in the chicken, egg products, and beefburgers eaten everywhere[19]. If you were a woman with your soon-to-be-born son or daughter developing in your uterus, how much estrogen would you want to wash through his or her brain and genital tissues as they are forming? A cheeseburger and milkshake lunch can create that very effect.

7. The current American diet, laden with animal fats (especially found in fast foods - cheeseburgers, milkshakes, fried chicken, pizza, etc.) begins to **clog the arteries** in childhood, setting the stage for heart attacks, strokes, and obesity[20]. The epidemiologic study performed by the Department of Medicine, Louisiana State University Medical Center, showed yellow, fatty streaks and cholesterol accumulations, both significant signs of early atherosclerotic clogging of the arteries in most children under age five - some even as young as nine months![21]

Thus, there are many reasons why the pregnant woman should consider not ingesting animal flesh and dairy products. Trading animal flesh for grain and legume protein, and exchanging animal fats for plant oils, are good bargains for both mother and child. Helping children develop preferences for food free of animal fat will assist in creating a lifetime gift of a lean, healthy body, with clean arteries and a lower risk of cancer[22,96,119,120].

With increasing frequency, studies are appearing in the scientific literature reporting that people on an animal-free (**vegan**) diet live longer, healthier lives[23],[36-42]. The direction of today's dietary evolution appears clear: the less animal foods eaten, the better. A growing number of health professionals believe that none is best, and **PREGNANCY, CHILDREN, and the VEGAN DIET** is offered as a guide towards instituting this healthful nutritional approach.

Chapter 2

VEGAN NUTRITION DURING PREGNANCY

THE HUMAN BODY HAS NO NUTRITIONAL REQUIREMENTS FOR ANIMAL FLESH OR COW'S MILK. IT FUNCTIONS SUPERBLY WITHOUT THEM, AND THIS INCLUDES PRODUCING HEALTHY OFFSPRING![33a]

Current understandings of human nutrition have antiquated the time-honored advice to "eat lots of meat and dairy products, so the baby gets enough protein and calcium". It is important to have an adequate intake of protein and calcium during pregnancy; however, meat and dairy products are certainly not the only sources of these nutrients. All the protein and calcium required for human health, including during pregnancy and childraising, are available in the delicious foods that grow from the earth.

Let's consider what the human body requires for proper nutrition each day, and explore why vegan foods work so well as a dietary "fuel", including during pregnancy.

NUTRITIONAL REQUIREMENTS

The average person, adult or child, pregnant or not, requires each day sufficient amounts of these six types of nutrients to run his or her body:

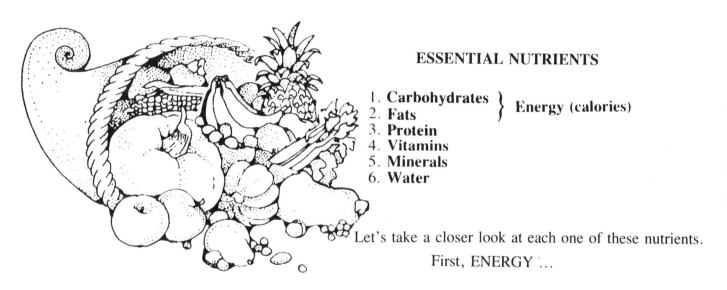

ESSENTIAL NUTRIENTS

1. **Carbohydrates** ⎫ **Energy (calories)**
2. **Fats** ⎬
3. **Protein** ⎭
4. **Vitamins**
5. **Minerals**
6. **Water**

Let's take a closer look at each one of these nutrients.

First, ENERGY ...

1, 2. **ENERGY** - Like a car requires gasoline to run, the body requires "fuel" for energy, so it can do its work of muscle contraction, nerve impulse conduction, hormone production, wound repair, cell growth, etc., and of course, its role in "constructing" the new baby. This "cell fuel" is composed of the **carbohydrates and oils** made by plants, from sunlight, air and water. It appears in the vegan diet as **sugars, starches and vegetable oils**. These fuels are found in abundance in **grains, vegetables, nuts, cooking oils, fruits**, etc.; it's easy for the pregnant woman to get enough each day if she enjoys her pastas, potatoes and fruit smoothies - and they're **not** fattening. Carbohydrates are "burned" for energy, while the animal fats tend to be stored in the body's fat depots.

3. **PROTEIN** - The "building block" material for making muscles, blood, hormones, hair, fingernails, immune antibodies, and, of course, the baby. The individual "building blocks" are called **amino acids**, and all that are required by the body are found in abundance in **grains, legumes, green vegetables, nuts, and seeds**.

4. **VITAMINS** - Our body cells do their work of protein production and metabolism by using active chemical substances called **enzymes**. These enzymes, the "machinery of life", require **vitamins** to perform their vital chemistry. The function of vitamins in your body, in relation to their enzyme "partners", is similar to the oil and lubricants in your car that permit the moving parts to work properly. Vitamins are "co-factors" for the enzymes, and essential to human health.

There are two families of vitamins, a) those that dissolve in **water**, and b) those that dissolve in **oil**.

The **water soluble vitamins** - which are not stored in the body, and thus must be consumed every day - include vitamin C, the B Complex, and Folic Acid. These vitamins are found in **green, leafy vegetables**, as well as in **citrus fruits** and **nutritional yeast**.

The **oil soluble vitamins** - which are stored in the liver, and thus need be consumed only several times per week - include Vitamins A and E. They are abundantly found in **yellow vegetables**, like carrots, squash, sweet potatoes, as well as in **melons** (and **some dark green leafies**, like kale and broccoli).

Thus, **fresh fruits and vegetables** hold the key to **vitamin** nutrition for the vegan.

5. **MINERALS** - Earth elements like potassium, sodium, iron, zinc, selenium, calcium, and iodine, are required for electrical and chemical reactions in the body. These metals are abundant in **green leafy vegetables, grains, mushrooms, nutritional yeast,** and in **sea vegetables** (kombu, kelp, dulse, nori, etc.) which can be added to soups, salads, etc.

6. Sufficient pure **WATER** is needed so that the blood flows, the glands secrete vital fluids, and the chemical reactions of life can occur in the cells. The state of pregnancy is a "watery" one, and the pregnant woman requires extra water for making additional blood for herself, the baby, and the three to six quarts of amniotic fluid in her uterus. She should try to drink at least four to six eight-ounce glasses per day in the form of **pure water, fruit juices, or vegetable juices**. The balance of water needed (total - 2 to 3 quarts daily) can be obtained from the **watery fruits, vegetables, soups and salads**, which are abundant in vegan cuisine.

That's it. Give the body sufficient amounts of these six nutrients, along with pleasant daily walks in the sunshine, and generous amounts of laughter, and the mother and baby will grow strong, healthy and balanced.

The "Basic Four Food Groups" classification, invented by the United States Department of Agriculture in 1956, is a concept that promotes the sale of meat and dairy products, but provides little guidance for healthful human nutrition. Animal flesh and cow's milk are certainly **not essential** for human health, and medical evidence is indicating that we can actually be healthier without them.

Hollywood screen actor, vegan, LEAF PHOENIX, age 9 years.

The nutritional requirements for human health just presented can all be conveniently (and safely) met by consuming ample portions each day from the "food families" of the "Vegan Six" Food Groups that follow. Balance in the vegan diet is achieved by eating the appropriate number of servings of each of the "Vegan Six." Pregnant women should try to eat the higher number of recommended servings.

"THE VEGAN SIX" FOOD GROUPS

<table>
<tr><td>1. WHOLE GRAINS and POTATOES</td><td>4. NUTS and SEEDS</td></tr>
<tr><td>2. LEGUMES</td><td>5. FRUITS</td></tr>
<tr><td>3. GREEN and YELLOW VEGETABLES</td><td>6. VITAMIN and MINERAL FOODS</td></tr>
</table>

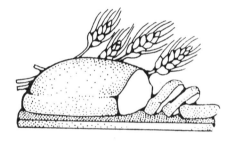  

1. **WHOLE GRAINS** and **STARCHES** - including **GRAIN PRODUCTS** and **POTATOES** - Whole grain brown rice, corn, millet, barley, bulghur, buckwheat groats, oats (including oatmeal, granola and other cereals), wheat (including cereals, breads, pastas, flour, etc.), amaranth, triticale, quinoa.

Nutrients - Energy, protein, oils, vitamins, and fiber

(for normal bowel function).

Quantity - 2-4 (4 ounce) servings daily

2. **LEGUMES** - (Anything that grows in a pod) - Green peas, lentils, chickpeas (garbanzos), beans of all types (navy, lima, kidney, aduki, etc.), soybeans and soy products (soy milk, tofu, texturized vegetable protein granules, tempeh, etc.), and sprouted seeds and legumes, such as alfalfa and mung.

Nutrients - Protein and oils.

Quantity - 1-2 (4 ounce) servings daily

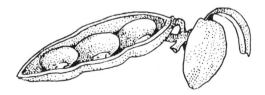

3. GREEN AND YELLOW VEGETABLES

Green - Broccoli, collards, kale, brussel sprouts, spinach, alfalfa sprouts, swiss chard, cabbage, romaine, cucumbers, mustard greens, endive, etc.

Yellow - Carrots, squash (acorn, hubbard, summer, spaghetti, etc.), sweet potatoes, pumpkins, parsnips, etc.

Nutrients - Vitamins, minerals, protein.

Quantity - 1-3 (4 ounce) servings daily

4. NUTS AND SEEDS - Almonds, walnuts, peanuts, pecans, filberts, macadamias, and nut butters made from these. Sesame seeds (and tahini butter made from them), sunflower seeds, pumpkin seeds.

Nutrients - Protein, oils, calcium, trace minerals.
Quantity - 1-3 (1 ounce) servings daily

5. FRUITS of all kinds, especially citrus and melons.

Nutrients - Energy, vitamins and minerals.
Quantity - 3-6 pieces daily

6. VITAMIN and MINERAL FOODS - For trace minerals and vitamin B-12.

(a) **Trace minerals**, like iodine, manganese, copper, etc., are found in **sea vegetables**, like kombu, dulse, kelp, nori, arame, wakame, and spirulina.
(b) A reliable **Vitamin B-12** source must be included at least three times weekly. Some convenient sources are B-12 fortified cereals, soy milks, soy "meat" products, texturized vegetable protein (TVP), etc.
or
a Vitamin B-12 supplement (liquid, or crushed B-12 tablets) which can be added to salad dressings, smoothies, etc.

Quantity - 1 serving of (a) and (b), at least 3 times weekly.

Because the "Vegan Six" consists of fresh, whole foods, there are many delicious treasures to be found in vegan cuisine. Let's consider some examples of "real" vegan food, and then look at some foods made from the "Vegan Six" that supply the most important nutrients.

REAL FOODS

Breakfast Favorites:

How about starting your day on a naturally sweet note with a generous fruit bowl of your favorites, like sliced peaches, apples, pears, plums, (U.S. grown) bananas, melons, and berries. Top with fruit juice and shredded coconut.

For those who prefer a more substantial breakfast, consider a stack of whole grain pancakes with real maple syrup, or a bowl of hot oatmeal, topped with raisins and sunflower seeds, and a dash of cinnamon.

HINT - Use a teaspoon of olive oil in place of melted butter, use maple syrup or malt barley syrup for sweetener, and use soy or sunflower milk in place of dairy cream or milk. (See Appendix V - Dairy Substitutes.)

For former scrambled egg fans, a plate of golden tofu "omelette", Western style, with chopped red and green peppers and onions, is easy to learn, quick to make, and cholesterol-free.

Baked, sliced plantains, with corn or bran muffins and fruit spread, creates a carbohydrate and fiber-rich breakfast, with a tropical touch.

Cold breakfast cereals, like granola, corn, or wheat flakes, made from the whole grain, are hearty and delicious, and can be topped with fruit, and sweet vanilla soymilk or blender-made sunflower milk.

Whole grain toast, with peanut butter and fruit spread, is an favorite "instant breakfast", high in protein and energy.

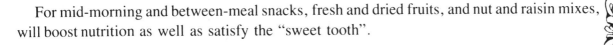

Snacks

For mid-morning and between-meal snacks, fresh and dried fruits, and nut and raisin mixes, will boost nutrition as well as satisfy the "sweet tooth".

Lunch

Open your refrigerator or lunchbox and warm up the delicately seasoned "veggie-grain burger" on a whole wheat bun with lettuce, tomatoes, sprouts, and "all the trimmings." A fresh green salad with non-dairy French dressing, and a thermos of last night's vegetable bean soup, balance the meal. A chocolately carob brownie makes a sweet dessert.

Dinner

A hearty, easy-to-make vegetable soup and/or green salad can again precede the entree.

Satisfying salads include: coleslaw, potato salad, carrot salad, and tofu "eggless" salad.

Full-bodied soups can feature: split pea, beet borscht, Scotch carrot/barley, tomato gazpacho, vegetable bean.

The main dish entree, which is based upon grains and/or potatoes, can display the colorful and tasty vegetarian tradition from countries around the globe, such as these:

From Italy, enjoy Meatless Lasagna, Eggplant Milanese, or Spaghetti and Tofu Balls.

How about Oriental Stir-Fried Vegetables with Cashews, served over rice or noodles?

An evening in "old Mexico" can begin with Corn Enchilladas or Tacos with Beans, or a spicy "Chili con Tofu."

A Mediterranean flavor can be created with Chickpea Hummus and chopped vegetables in whole wheat pocket pita bread.

Of course, there are delicious sauces and gravies to add flavor to most every dish.

Beverages

Healthful options for drinking include pure water, fruit juices, tea and coffee-style beverages. Non-dairy milks and fruit smoothies can be enjoyed between meals. (See Appendix V).

Desserts

Fresh fruits, eaten at least an hour after the main course, should usually serve as dessert, but versatile vegan cuisine offers many sweet treats, like apple pie, carob cookies, Danish pastry, tofu "cheesecake", as well as non-dairy "nice cream", yogurt, puddings, and candies.

As you can begin to see, a diet free of meat and dairy products is far from austere. People who really love to eat, will find plenty in vegan cuisine to love.

Sample menus for two complete days of vegan meals, including numerical nutritional analyses, will soon be presented, showing that one can meet or exceed all the U.S. Recommended Daily Allowances (R.D.A.'s) on a balanced vegan diet.

People who are sensitive or have actual allergies to soy products, should substitute chickpeas, lentils, peas, or other legumes for soy foods such as tofu, tempeh, soy milk, etc.

People who are sensitive or have actual allergies to wheat, should choose pastas and breads, made from rice, barley, or other grain flours.

How to NOURISH a HEALTHY Human Being, VEGAN Style

It is valuable to remember that the human digestive system, with its grinding molar teeth and long intestines, is ideally engineered to digest a plant-based diet. Remember, some of the strongest animals on Earth, from thorough-bred horses to mighty elephants, grow to full size and raise healthy offspring entirely on vegan fare. They never eat meat or cheese, nor do they take nutrition courses. They also do not get high blood pressure, osteoporosis, clogged arteries, and other scourges of meat-eating Western society.

Herbivorous animals naturally eat a wide variety of plant foods, containing grains, legumes, greens, vegetables and fruits. The good news is that the food formula that works so well for them, works for us, too!

People eating in the vegan style soon experience their bodies becoming more balanced, and they intuitively feel that animal-free foods are the best for them. For those who examine nutrition "by the numbers", here are the nutritional "credentials" of the vegan diet.

THE NUMBERS GAME

The average **non·pregnant** adult requires each day:

PROTEIN: 56 grams for males
                  (the weight of 18 pennies)

                  44 grams for females
                  (the weight of 15 pennies)

CALCIUM: 800 milligrams

IRON: 18 milligrams

The **pregnant** woman requires each day an **additional:**

30 grams of PROTEIN   (total - 74 grams protein)
                       (the weight of 25 pennies)

400 mgs of CALCIUM   (total - 1200 milligrams calcium)

12 - 42 mgs of IRON   (total - 30-60 milligrams iron)

The **lactating** woman has the same calcium and iron needs as the pregnant woman, but needs only 20 additional grams of protein.

The young mother or mother-to-be has a right to know for certain whether she can meet all her nutritional needs from plant-derived foods. Most nutritional concerns for pregnant women center on the additional need for **protein, minerals** like **calcium, iron** and **zinc**, and vitamins such as B-12, D, and **folic acid**.

Let's see how each of these nutrient needs can be conveniently

and efficiently met with vegan food sources only...

I. PROTEIN

"Getting enough protein", that perennial question posed to vegetarians, is not a worry with a balanced vegan diet. All plants, especially **grains, legumes, green vegetables, nuts, and seeds**, contain high quality protein that will fill all the body's needs, especially when eaten in combination with each other.

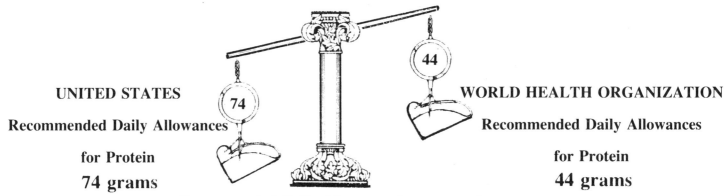

UNITED STATES

Recommended Daily Allowances

for Protein

74 grams

WORLD HEALTH ORGANIZATION

Recommended Daily Allowances

for Protein

44 grams

Recommended Daily Allowance for pregnant women

The current United States R.D.A. values used in this book, 74 grams daily - the weight of 25 pennies - is well above that amount truly necessary for a healthy pregnancy, and that of childbearing period. The World Health Organization is probably more realistic in their recommendations of 44 grams of protein daily during pregnancy, and 39 grams daily during lactation.[56]

However, for the relatively short duration of pregnancy, there may be an advantage to a high-protein intake, especially in the later months of pregnancy.

The condition of fluid retention and high blood pressure, called **preeclampsia**, or "toxemia of pregnancy," has been attributed to insufficient protein intake. Medical studies on 775 vegan mothers show them to be less prone to this serious condition, possibly due to the protein content and other nutritional factors (less arachidonic acid, etc.) inherent in the vegan diet [56a]. Therefore, a diet rich in protein-containing foods, especially in the final trimester of pregnancy, is a prudent strategy.

Thus, the higher U.S. R.D.A. of 74 grams of protein per day will be accepted and used in examples, instead of the World Health Organization's lower recommendations. Enjoy more nut mixes, tofu sandwiches, bean/barley soups, and steamed greens!

Protein Complementing? - Relax...

The idea of plant protein being "incomplete," and lacking some amino acids, has been shown to be a myth[57]. Nature simply does not make a soybean, potato, or grain of wheat, without using **all** the same amino acids (the "building blocks" of protein) required by the metabolism of humans[58]. Rice, corn, potatoes, and wheat, have all been shown to keep people in positive protein balance, even when used as the sole protein source[59].

Although combinations of any of the major protein foods do increase the quality and amount of usable protein, it has become evident that it is **not necessary** to "combine" proteins at each meal. Francis Moore Lappe', who brought "protein complementing" to public attention in her landmark book, DIET FOR A SMALL PLANET,* now recognizes that intentional protein "complementing" is unnecessary, and states so in the most recent revision of that work. As nutritional scientists have come to recognize, the protein from the whole grain toast enjoyed at breakfast, as well as the tofu in the dinner casserole, are "complete" in their own right and will each find their way to your liver and other tissues in the right proportions, and be well utilized.

However, the more variety in protein sources, the better, because your body tissues should have the widest variety of amino acid "building blocks" with which to work. Combining protein-rich ingredients does increase the nutritional value of a dish or meal significantly, and useful combinations that increase protein variety are given in the **"PROTEIN PYRAMID"**.

*Ballantine Books, 101 Fifth Avenue, New York, NY 10003

To provide examples for help in meal planning (and not to cause worry about possible protein deficiency), some classic high-protein combinations from vegan cuisine are diagramed in the following "Protein Pyramid." These protein-rich foods will replace meat and dairy products in the human diet, while avoiding the burden of saturated animal fats and other adulterants.

Two ample helpings of any of these combinations average 15 to 35 grams of high quality protein, and thus will provide a large measure of the daily requirements for a pregnant woman or a growing child. Served with green vegetables, soy milks, and other high protein foods, these entree ideas are nutritious substitutes for meat and will help create "protein security" for the pregnant woman.

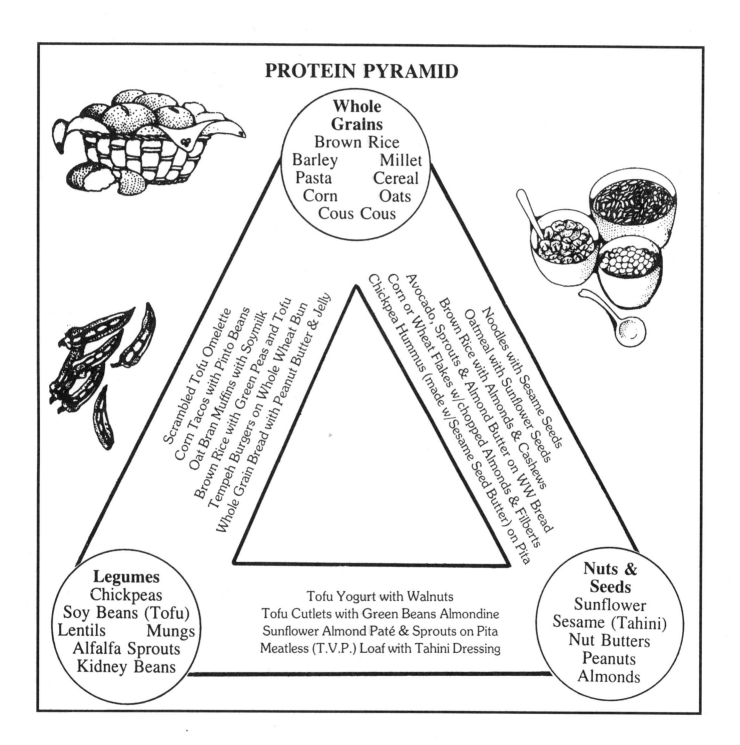

PROTEIN PYRAMID

Whole Grains
Brown Rice
Barley   Millet
Pasta   Cereal
Corn   Oats
Cous Cous

Scrambled Tofu Omelette
Corn Tacos with Pinto Beans
Oat Bran Muffins with Soymilk
Brown Rice with Green Peas and Tofu
Tempeh Burgers on Whole Wheat Bun
Whole Grain Bread with Peanut Butter & Jelly

Noodles with Sesame Seeds
Oatmeal with Sunflower Seeds
Brown Rice with Almonds & Cashews
Avocado, Sprouts & Almond Butter on WW Bread
Corn or Wheat Flakes w/chopped Almonds & Filberts
Chickpea Hummus (made w/Sesame Seed Butter) on Pita

Legumes
Chickpeas
Soy Beans (Tofu)
Lentils   Mungs
Alfalfa Sprouts
Kidney Beans

Tofu Yogurt with Walnuts
Tofu Cutlets with Green Beans Almondine
Sunflower Almond Paté & Sprouts on Pita
Meatless (T.V.P.) Loaf with Tahini Dressing

Nuts & Seeds
Sunflower
Sesame (Tahini)
Nut Butters
Peanuts
Almonds

13

The pregnant woman learning about vegan nutrition should take encouragement from the experience at an intentional community in Tennessee (The Farm). A published medical study of almost eight hundred vegan women there revealed that they had normal pregnancies and bore full term, normal weight infants[56A]. These women were health-conscious, received good prenatal care, supplemented their diets with prenatal vitamins, calcium, and iron, and took extra care to assure a good protein intake

The meals these women prepared for themselves and their families accented the following "Protein All-Stars," which are "foundation foods" from the first four of the "Vegan Six." The members of the "Protein All-Star" team listed below are so rich in protein, that one cannot design a 2,000 calorie diet based upon appropriate amounts of these foods, without getting more than adequate "complete protein"[54,60]. Eating three balanced vegan meals a day, styled after those presented in the food plans, will guarantee that the R.D.A. for protein is met.

Thus, these "Protein All-Stars" are important foods for the pregnant woman to become familiar with and learn to enjoy frequently.

PROTEIN ALL-STARS

GRAINS -Brown rice, oats (cereals - oatmeal, granola, etc.) millet, corn, barley, bulghur, wheat (including whole wheat bread, pastas, cereals, flour, etc.)

LEGUMES -Green peas, lentils, chick peas, alfalfa sprouts, mung beans and beans of all kinds (kidney, lima, aduki, navy beans, soy beans and products made from them; e.g., tofu, texturized vegetable protein granules, tempeh, soy milks, etc.)

GREENS -Broccoli, collards, kale, kohlrabi, spinach, dark green lettuce, endive, romaine, beet and mustard greens, okra, zucchini squash, swiss chard, etc.

NUTS & SEEDS -Almonds,cashews,walnuts,peanuts, filberts, pistachios, pecans, macadamias - and nut butters made from these. Sunflower seeds, sesame seeds (including tahini butter made from ground sesame seeds), pumpkin seeds, etc.

SPROUTS

No discussion of protein would be complete without mentioning the wonderful nutritive value of sprouts. All seeds, grains, and legumes can (and some people say should) be sprouted or at least soaked overnight before their use in meal preparation. The soaking/sprouting process vastly increases the content of usable protein, and raises the active vitamin content by several hundred per cent[60]. The digestibility of beans and seeds also improves greatly as the enzymes activated by the sprouting process change the starches to simple sugars. Alfalfa and mung bean sprouts, easily created in a jar on your kitchen window sill, or purchased at the supermarket, serve as nutritious garnishes to salads and sandwiches.

Kids seem to love sprouts, and thrive on the nutrients they contain. In fact, sprouting is a fine educational project that children can do themselves, and will teach them to value and enjoy the miracle of growing food. Pregnant women find them especially palatable, as well. Instructions for sprouting, as well as recipe ideas, are found in most vegetarian cookbooks, health food stores, and are available from the vegetarian societies listed at the end of this book.

Resist the temptation to eat more than 2 ounces of sprouts daily. There are plant alkaloids, especially in alfalfa sprouts, that may adversely affect the mother and baby if eaten in **excessive** amounts.

Hopefully, this section has allayed any case of "protein panic," and has increased your confidence in the nutritional adequacy of the vegan diet. Next, let's consider some "elemental" ideas about - Minerals.

II. MINERALS

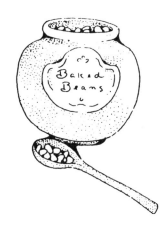

Like all other animals on Earth, every cell in our body requires metallic elements from the Earth's crust in order to function properly. Three minerals, **calcium, iron,** and **zinc**, are of special importance to the pregnant woman.

CALCIUM

This vital element is required for healthy function of muscle, blood, and bone, in both the mother and the fetus. With proper menu selection, the pregnant woman's dietary needs for calcium can be met by the wide variety of calcium-rich foods in vegan cuisine.

The whole foods of the vegan diet listed in Appendix I, especially **green, leafy vegetables**, and **legumes**, like beans, lentils, garbanzos and tofu*, are particularly rich in calcium, as are **sesame seed butter** (tahini), sunflower **seeds** and **nuts**. These foods should and do appear frequently in a balanced vegan diet, and three balanced vegan meals daily should easily supply 800 to 1000 milligrams of calcium, especially if calcium-fortified soymilk is utilized.*[123a]

If "calcium insurance" is desired, to assure meeting the 1200 milligrams of the U.S. Recommended Daily Allowance, a supplement of an additional 500 milligrams of calcium, preferably in the "lactate gluconate" or "ascorbate" form - that means the calcium is coupled with Vitamin C - should be employed. Combined with the minimum of 900 milligrams of calcium consumed daily in the foods in the Sample Meal plans - not to mention the substantial amounts of calicum frequently present in drinking water - the 1200 milligrams of calcium recommended by the R.D.A.'s is easily achieved.

A liquid or powder preparation, mixed in juice and sipped throughout the day, would be the gentlest and most efficient way to ingest the calcium. Tablets are less well absorbed than liquid.

For proper mineral balance, the 500 milligrams of calcium should also be combined with 200 to 300 miligrams of **magnesium** - read the label on the supplement package to see how much magnesium is present. Such a mineral supplement is prudent for most pregnant women, and thus is recommended. Often, some calcium and magnesium is included in standard prenatal vitamin supplements - again, become a wise consumer and be a reader of labels.

If calcium supplements are used be sure that they are **NOT** made from **bone meal, dolomite,** or **oyster shell**. These substances are **often contaminated** with arsenic, lead or mercury that accumulates in the bones and shells of these animals.[82-84]

*Calcium values calculated on "Nutrition Wizard"™, Center for Science and Public Interest, Washington, D. C. 20036.

Some nutritionists have expressed concern that all the calcium that is eaten may not be absorbed from the intestine into the bloodstream, as it may be bound to other substances in the plant, such as oxalic or phytic acid. Thus, it was felt the actual amount of (usable) calcium might be lower than the amounts listed in some nutritional tables for oxalate-rich vegetables such as spinach, swiss chard, cashews and almonds.

Fortunately, this calcium-inhibiting effect is proving to be more theoretical than real, as calcium deficiency from inadequate dietary intake is quite rare[83]. Apparently, on a more natural human diet, based on whole plant foods, and containing only moderate protein and calcium, the wonderful human intestine becomes more efficient at absorbing calcium.

However, to be sure, use plenty of **greens** like **broccoli, collards, kale, mustard, turnips, celery, and romaine lettuce, and roots** like **turnips and carrots**, which are rich in calcium and relatively free of these binding substances. These vegetables are among the best "usable calcium providers" in all of vegan cuisine. They should appear frequently in the diet of all pregnant women, (and anyone else who desires an adequate calcium intake) in the form of salads, casseroles, and steamed side dishes.

Because calcium (and water-soluble vitamins) often leach out into the water used to cook or steam greens, this cooking water makes a calcium-rich stock for soups, salad dressings and vegetable stews, and thus should be saved.

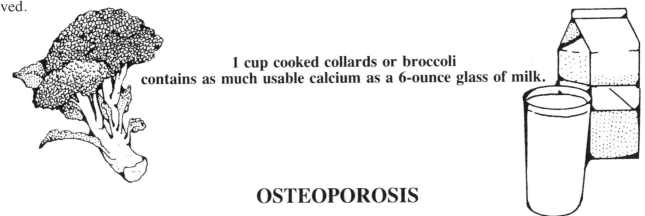

1 cup cooked collards or broccoli contains as much usable calcium as a 6-ounce glass of milk.

OSTEOPOROSIS

OSTEOPOROSIS - Calcium Deficiency or Protein Excess?

Americans are told to eat more calcium than anyone else on Earth, to prevent **osteoporosis**. This condition of weakened bones that fracture easily is actually promoted by the slow, steady loss of body calcium through the urine. This calcium loss occurs for hours after one eats a meal containing concentrated protein, like meat, poultry and fish. This occurs because the kidneys must lose calcium as they cleanse the blood of excess protein waste ("protein-induced hypercalciuria")[55,72].

The United States and the Scandinavian countries consume more protein, including dairy products, than any other nation. Their people suffer higher rates of osteoporosis than in any other countries[71]. These findings not only underscore the threat of excessive protein in the diet, but indicate that consuming dairy products offers no protection against osteoporosis, probably due to the high protein content of milk.

(In comparing ethnic groups, the Eskimos, with their fish and meat-laden diet, are the osteoporosis "champions")[72].

By healthy contrast, medical studies show osteoporosis to be uncommon in well-nourished vegans who are physically active[81]. The vegan style of nutrition, free of meat's burdensome protein loads, creates less calcium loss from the body.[123b] Non-pregnant vegans seem to do well on 600 to 800 mgs. of calcium daily. However, as discussed, the pregnant woman should be extra generous with calcium-containing foods and try to exceed 1000 mgs. of calcium daily, using supplements, if necessary.

IRON

The needs for **iron** are increased during pregnancy because both the infant and the mother are busy creating new blood.

Notice, however, the great **range of increase** of the Recommended Daily Allowance for iron. From the non-pregnant requirement of 18 mgs. per day, an **additional 12 to 42 mgs.** is recommended. The meaning of this large variation is that there exists large differences among women in **efficiency of absorption** of iron from the intestine into the bloodstream.

That is, some women absorb into their bloodstream a large fraction of the iron they eat in food, and some absorb lesser amounts. Ten (10%) per cent is a usual "absorption fraction" for iron.

We will discuss iron-containing foods next, as well as ideas for increasing the fraction of iron absorbed. However, one thing is apparent: eating red meat is no insurance against developing anemia (too little red blood), as **most** pregnant (and non-pregnant) women who develop iron deficiency anemia eat red meat! They also may be drinking cow's milk and eating dairy products, both of which have been shown to inhibit the absorption of iron. [84a] The use of dairy products also "crowds out" greens and other iron-rich plant foods that should appear in a balanced diet for adults.

The R.D.A.'s of 30 - 60 milligrams of iron (that's a lot for **any** diet to supply from food sources alone) imply that **all** pregnant women should take iron supplements. This should not be necessary.

Women who are "good absorbers" of iron will get sufficient amounts from foods like **green leafy vegetables, raisins, whole grains**, (wheat, oats, barley, millet, corn, rice, etc., and foods made from them, like whole grain breads, pastas, cereals, granola, etc.), **nuts, seeds, legumes, sorghum molasses, and dried fruits** (apricots, etc.).

Very importantly, **Vitamin C** markedly increases the absorption of iron from the food into the body: so **green leafy vegetables (which abound in the vegan diet, and contain both** iron and vitamin C) are **especially valuable foods during pregnancy**. Sixty milligrams of vitamin C increases the absorption of the iron in corn by five times! Thus, vitamin C-containing foods - **turnip greens, brocoli, brussels sprouts, potatoes, sweet potatoes, peppers, tomatoes**, and **cabbage** - are especially good to combine with iron-rich foods.

In summary, the prevention, detection and treatment of anemia is a **clinical** situation, different for each woman, depending on her efficiency of absorption of iron. Therefore, it is difficult and unwise to try to adhere to an "ironclad rule" about supplementation for every woman. Excess iron tablets can cause stomach irritation and can actually be toxic to mother and fetus[85].

A suitable strategy for assuring iron adequacy on a vegan diet would be:

1. Accentuation of the iron and Vitamin C-rich foods listed above; and

2. Good communication and cooperation with the health care practitioner (physician, nurse-midwife, etc.), with a commitment to responsible prenatal care.

3. Determination of the woman's hemoglobin value at the beginning of pregnancy, and checked via "finger-stick" blood count, at four to eight-week intervals (with more frequent determinations performed, if necessary, as the pregnancy progresses).

a. If the hemoglobin value is staying above 14 grams/dl, the woman is staying in positive iron balance on her dietary intake of iron alone, and no tablet supplementation is needed.

b. A fall of the hemoglobin towards 12 gm/dl is a cause for concern, and an indication to increase the iron and Vitamin C containing foods in the diet. Cooking in cast iron skillets and pots has been shown to be an effective method of raising the iron content of cooked foods[86].

c. Re-check the hemoglobin level in 2 to 4 weeks, and if dietary maneuvers are not successful in halting the falling hemoglobin values then iron supplementation is indicated.

Ferrous gluconate with vitamin C added is probably the most effective and well-tolerated form of iron supplement, but the formulation with which the supervising health care person is most experienced should be the one of choice. **Total** iron supplementation should be limited to 60 milligrams of elemental iron daily.

You may notice that **iron-containing foods** (accenting dark leafy greens and dried fruits) **are also among the foods presented as rich sources of calcium and folic acid**. As a rule of thumb, in vegan meal planning:

Eat to obtain sufficient protein and energy (calories).

This means, **emphasize grains, legumes, fruits, nuts, and seeds,**
with plenty of **green and yellow vegetables**.

Then, the needs for vitamins, minerals, and essential fatty acids,
with the exceptions of vitamins B-12 and D, will also be met.

With responsible prenatal care and appropriate meal planning, anemia from iron deficiency should not occur.

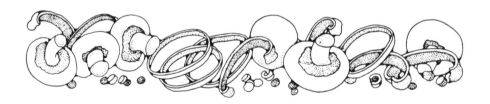

ZINC

Zinc is essential for the health of the pregnant woman and the developing baby in her womb. Fortunately, zinc is found in **whole grains, green leafy vegetables, mushrooms, nuts, seeds (especially sesame/tahini), legumes, tofu, miso, wheat germ, nutritional yeast,** and **fortified cereals**. These foods should meet all the woman's needs for zinc. However, to provide extra zinc "insurance", a prenatal vitamin/mineral taken every day or two should contain 15 to 30 milligrams of elemental zinc.

III. VITAMINS

The vitamins necessary for human health, except B-12 and D - more about them next - are found in fresh **dark green leafy vegetables**, in **yellow vegetables**, as well as in many **fruits**.

Enjoying ample amounts of fresh garden salads, raw and steamed green and yellow vegetables, and fresh fruits, holds the key to "vitamin insurance."

At this time, examine the table that follows, to build your confidence in the abundance of vitamins in natural, whole foods.

WHERE THE VITAMINS ARE

For healthy cell metabolism in nerve, muscle and blood, your body needs two "families" of vitamins: those that dissolve in water, and those that dissolve in oil.

VITAMINS

WATER SOLUBLE
(Not stored - needed daily)

The "B Complex":
    B-1 (Thiamine)
    B-2 (Riboflavin)
    B-6 (Pyridoxine)
    Choline
    Biotin
    Folic Acid
    Others of "B Complex"
    Vitamin C

Found in:

Green Vegetables
    Alfalfa Sprouts
    Avocadoes
    Beans (green)
    Broccoli   Bokchoy
    Brussels Sprouts
    Cabbage family
    Collards
    Cucumbers   Endive
    Kale   Leeks
    Mustard Greens
    Peppers
    Romaine Lettuce
    Spinach
    Sprouts (mung bean, etc.)
    Swiss Chard
    Turnip Greens

Nutritional Yeast (Vit. B-12)

Fruits
    Melons - cantelope, honeydew, etc.,
        (also contain Vitamin A)
    Citrus - oranges, grapefruits, etc.,
        (for Vitamin C)

FAT SOLUBLE
(Stored in your liver - needed 3 to 5 times a week)

Vitamin A
Vitamin E
Essential Fatty Acids (EFA's)

Found in:

Yellow Vegetables and Oil-Rich Foods
    Carrots
    Corn
    Pumpkin
    Rutabagas
    Squash:
        Acorn
        Butternut
        Hubbard
        Spaghetti
        Summer
    Sweet Potatoes
    Almonds
    Corn Oil
    Linseed Oil
        (food grade for EFA's)
    Safflower Oil
    Sunflower Seeds
    Sesame Seeds
        (tahini)

Whole Grains

The inclusion of these fresh fruits and vegetables should greatly reduce, if not eliminate completely, the need for vitamin supplements. If a woman wanted to rely solely on the naturally occurring vitamins from the fresh fruits and vegetables in her diet, she could probably do so with little risk to herself or to her baby. After all, women have been giving birth and raising healthy babies long before vitamin supplements were invented.

Ideally, fresh, inexpensive, locally grown organic produce, cultivated in healthy, fertile soil, would be available to all of us. If one enjoys daily steamed green and yellow vegetables, as well as a generous garden green salad that includes fresh, dark, leafy greens, a few carrots and a strip of dulse (or other sea vegetable) for trace minerals, all vitamin (see "B-12" section) and mineral needs (see Calcium, below) should be met adequately and deliciously.

The main rationale for a vegan woman to use supplements would be to provide "insurance" if she questions the freshness or quality of the produce in her meals. The vitamin content of most vegetables decreases from the moment of harvest, and current commercial vegetable production utilizes long-term storage techniques to permit cross country transport of produce. Thus, a particular lettuce or green pepper may be many days old before it appears on the supermarket shelf, and may be lacking the needed vitamins.

Most women do live in cities, and are thus dependent upon fruits and vegetables with questionable vitamin content. Therefore, judicious use of prenatal vitamin supplementation is recommended.

It is prudent to remember that in the case of vitamins and minerals, as with protein, **more is not better - excessive amounts of vitamins A, D, B-6, and iron, can be toxic to both mother and fetus**[61]. The pregnant woman should take no more than one prenatal vitamin tablet daily, and, given the "vitamin wealth,, of the vegan diet, one tablet, two to three times weekly, is probably sufficient.

An appropriate vitamin supplement should contain the following nutrients in approximately these amounts:

Vitamin A	- 7,000 I.U. (Int. Units)	Vitamin D	- 400 I.U.
Vitamin E	- 15 I.U.	Vitamin C	- 100 mg.
Folic Acid	- 1 mg.	Niacin	- 15 mg.
Thiamin	- 1.5 mg.	Riboflavin	- 1.5 mg.
Vitamin B-6	- 5 mg.	Vitamin B-12	- 4 mcg.
Calcium	- 500 mg.	Iodine	- 100 mcg.
Iron	- 20 - 45 mg.	Magnesium	- 400 mg.
Zinc - 15 mgs.			

One Bronson Prenatal vitamin tablet daily meets the R.D.A. vitamin requirements, while being free from animal ingredients. (Bronson products are available through Bronson Pharmaceuticals, 4526 Rinetti Lane, La Canada, CA 91011-0628. This vitamin is recommended only on merit of its content and vegan nature; the author has no personal or financial connections with this or any other vitamin producer.)

VITAMINS OF SPECIAL INTEREST

VITAMIN B-12

Vitamin B-12: This vitamin is necessary for normal blood cell growth and nerve function. It is required in tiny amounts; an average of 3 **millionths** of a gram each day will suffice for all adults, pregnant or not, with proportionately less for children. The liver stores a three to five-year supply of vitamin B-12, and thus acts as a great "B-12 buffer" for the body. Consequently, there is no need to ingest the vitamin daily. Consuming vitamin B-12 (in its active form - cyanocobalamin) every few days, or even weekly, will suffice.

No animal **makes** vitamin B-12. It is made by **bacteria** that grow in the soil, and in fermented foods. Vitamin B-12 is found in beef liver and other flesh foods because the cow has eaten plants that have B-12-bearing soil particles clinging to them, as well as having consumed water containing the bacterially-made vitamin. The vitamin B-12 the cow eats is stored in her liver and muscles. It is true that to obtain vitamin B-12, one can kill the cow and eat her liver and muscles. However, there are gentler and less expensive sources for humans to obtain this nutrient.

Practicing vegans who do not take vitamin supplements seldom become deficient in vitamin B-12, probably because they obtain it from two subtle but important sources:

1. There are bacteria within the human body that make vitamin B-12, in the mouth's saliva, in the liver's bile, and within the intestinal contents [64,65]. Some, and perhaps many, vegans, may absorb the products of these natural "vitamin generators" that live within their own digestive systems. Thus, these people may internally meet their own B-12 requirements, and have no need for deriving any from the diet[65A].

2. The diet of today's vegan usually includes foods that have been **fortified** with vitamin B-12, such as enriched cereals, soy milks, soy-based meat analogs, and nutritional yeast*. The woman who is utilizing these fortified products regularly, (or is taking a standard prenatal vitamin supplement that contains vitamin B-12), should feel confident that she is satisfying her need for that vitamin.[66,122]

All pregnant women following vegan nutritional principles should assure that they have a reliable source of Vitamin B-12 in their diet and consume it at least daily.

If the woman's diet does not include B-12-fortified foods, nor prenatal multivitamin supplements, a 25-microgram tablet of vitamin B-12 (cyanocobalamin) should be taken at least three times weekly. A convenient way to assure adequate B-12 supplies for the entire family is to crush several 25 or 50-microgram vitamin B-12 tablets, and add small amounts of the powder to gravies, soy milks, fruit juices, and blender smoothies, several times per week. Sublingual supplements are both very convenient and effective.

Thus, the pregnant woman can easily obtain sufficient amounts of this vital substance without having to resort to meat, dairy products, or other animal foods "to get enough B-12."

It is important to read the label on the vitamin bottle to verify that the vitamin B-12 is derived from pure plant (bacterial) sources, rather than extracted from beef liver or other slaughterhouse products.

MEDICAL NOTE: A simple blood test can determine whether a person's vitamin B-12 level is adequate - (hypersegmented white blood cells, or a vitamin B-12 level below 150 picograms/ml are medical indications for B-12 supplementation).

*Nutritional yeast is a food yeast, grown on a B-12-enriched medium, and is a pleasant-tasting, yellow powder. It is a versatile cooking ingredient, and can be mixed into gravies, casseroles, and sprinkled on salads, steamed vegetables, etc., to give a "cheesy" taste and texture to these foods. One tablespoon is reported to contain up to 4 millionths of a gram of vitamin B-12. Most people, even those with "yeast sensitivity," can enjoy foods prepared with nutritional yeast. However, because the actual amount of vitamin B-12 in nutritional yeast may vary from batch to batch, this product should not be relied upon as the only vitamin B-12 source for pregnant women or growing children.

The same caveat applies to fermented foods such as tempeh, miso, and shoyu. As U. S. food production methods have become more sanitary, B-12 levels in fermented foods have been decreasing. They cannot be relied on as consistent sources of vitamin B-12.

KYLE CHIDESTER, at 2 1/2 years.

VITAMIN D

Vitamin D is not really a "vitamin" at all, but a hormone made within our own bodies. Vitamin D is made when **sunlight** falls upon our skin and activates a fatty substance called **ergosterol.** The ergosterol is transformed into active vitamin D, and as it flows in the blood through the wall of the small intestine, it permits us to absorb calcium from our food into our bloodstream. Thus, vitamin D is intimately connected with the calcium balance throughout the body, in the blood, in the muscles, and in the bones.

Sunlight is so effective in creating vitamin D, that 15 minutes of sunlight exposure on the face and arms is all that is required to meet our daily needs. Because vitamin D is stored in the liver, a summer of moderate sun exposure should create all the body's vitamin D supplies to carry it throughout the winter. If brief daily sun exposure is possible there should be no need to ingest vitamin D in our food."

For a pregnant woman living in very cold climates, adequate sunlight exposure in winter may be a problem. She should try to walk outside each day, or at least try sitting near an open window. If direct sun exposure is impractical, vitamin D supplementation, usually incorporated into the prenatal vitamin tablet, is advisable.

In meeting vitamin D needs through food sources (as opposed to sun exposure), 400 International Units (I.U.) of vitamin D per day is more than adequate for a pregnant woman. A supplement tablet should contain no more than this amount, because excessive vitamin D can be toxic to the mother and to the developing fetus[69].

Care should be taken to insure that the vitamin D is made from plant-derived sources (ergocalciferol) rather than from beef liver or fish liver oil (cholecalciferol). Be sure to read the label, or ask the pharmacist or health food store attendant, if there are questions about the vitamin source.

Incidentally, cow's milk does not naturally contain Vitamin D; it is added at the dairy. **Vitamin D-enriched soy milks** are available and can be included in the diet as a dairy substitute.

FOLIC ACID

This vitamin, necessary for proper development of the nervous system in the baby, is found abundantly in the vegan diet in **dark, green, leafy vegetables, nutritional yeast,** and **dates.** Thus, vegans typically exceed the one milligram daily requirement. Ample helpings of broccoli, kale, collards, or spinach, as well as one or two dried dates every few days, will insure the recommended one milligram daily intake throughout pregnancy. Be sure any prenatal vitamin supplement taken contains at least one milligram of folic acid (or "folate").

VITAMIN B-6

Necessary for many vital energy-producing reactions, as well as healthy nerves and mucus membranes, vitamin B-6 (pyridoxine) is found in **green vegetables, grains, legumes,** and **nutritional yeast.** Adequate supplies of vitamin B-6 on a balanced vegan diet are easy to obtain.

A good prenatal vitamin supplement should contain at least five (up to 25) milligrams, but excessive vitamin B-6 can be toxic to mother and fetus, so a total of 50 milligrams of vitamin B-6 should not be exceeded without guidance of a physician.

22

IV. FATS

ESSENTIAL FATTY ACIDS

The pregnant woman requires **fats** in her diet, (1) for an energy source, and (2) because she and her developing baby use fats to construct and maintain vital organs, such as the brain, heart, and kidneys. Fortunately, the only two fats **essential** for humans (**linoleic** and **linolenic acid**) abound in many plant sources - namely, **whole grains** and **legumes, avocados, nuts,** and **nut butters**, like almond, peanut, and sesame (tahini), as well as in **refined oils**, like olive, safflower, and flaxseed oils.

There is no nutritional reason why a pregnant woman must eat any fat derived from animals, and some very good reasons exist not to eat it. Animal fats, like the marbling in beef, the yellow streaks in chicken, the white flecks in sausages and lunchmeats, and the butterfat in cheese, ice cream, and other dairy products all tend to make the pregnant woman overweight. Excessive weight gain is a danger during pregnancy, as every extra pound raises the risk of diabetes[49], and high blood pressure[50], as well as delivery of overly large infants, who may suffer birth trauma, or require cesarean section for delivery[51].

If surgery becomes necessary for any reason, overweight patients suffer more complications during anesthesia and post-operative recovery[52].

Finally, though of no small importance to women who care about their appearance, the extra pounds gained during pregnancy from indulging in fatty foods while "eating for two", are notoriously difficult to shed after delivery.

As the vegan woman consumes no animal fats in her diet, she should view oil-containing whole plant foods, like nuts, seeds, and whole grains, as well as the judicious use of high-quality vegetable oils as aids in creating good health.

The best oil for daily use in salad dressings, baking recipes, etc., is olive oil, as it has a healthful balance of saturated and unsaturated fatty acids that is easy to metabolize, and is gentle on the arteries. Safflower oil is less expensive, and is also suitable for daily use. These oils can be used in cooking, as well as at the table for brushing onto baked potatoes or hot corn to take the place of (melted) butter or margarine.

Oils derived from cottonseed or rapeseed (canola oil) should be avoided, as they contain harmful contaminants, like gossypol, and erucic acid, which can damage the internal organs.

Oil should be purchased and stored in dark bottles to retard rancidity induced by light, and refrigerated after opening. The label on the oil bottle should state the oil is "cold-pressed", as this technique of oil extraction creates fewer harmful degradation products, like free radicals. The most **heat-stable** oils are the most saturated, like coconut and palm, which are thus suitable for the **small amount** used in stir-frying.

Products containing "partially hydrogenated" vegetable oils, especially commercial baked goods, chips, candies, etc., should be avoided completely, due to their unhealthful free radical content and unnatural "trans" configuration.

Vegan people usually have no difficulty in meeting their needs for essential fatty acids. If they do notice signs of oil deficiency, like dry skin, dandruff, seborrhea, lusterless hair, etc., they should increase the amounts of safflower and olive oils in their diet. Beware, however, of "over-oiling" your food.

V. CARBOHYDRATES

Getting enough **carbohydrates** for energy in the plant-based vegan diet is never a problem. **Grains, breads, pastas, legumes, seeds, nuts, fruits, and starchy vegetables**, abound with carbohybdrates and form the foundation of most meals. **Potatoes**, with their high-grade carbohydrate and moderate protein content, are almost "perfect foods". If you were stranded on a desert island, potatoes would be the best choice for your dietary staple. Carbohydrates are the friends of the pregnant woman and the developing baby.

Remember, carbohydrates are the main fuel burned by our body cells. Contrary to the myths about starches, foods rich in complex carbohydrates and fiber, like potatoes, whole grain breads, and pastas, will not make the pregnant woman overweight. One of the advantages of vegan cuisine is that one can enjoy **ample** quantities of delicious food without worrying about the waistline. Vegan mothers report that recovering their figure after childbirth is relatively easy.

VI. WATER

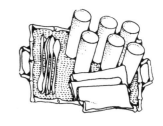

The state of pregnancy is a "watery" one. The pregnant woman requires extra water for making additional blood for herself and the baby, as well as the 3 to 6 quarts of amniotic fluid in the uterus. Pure **water** should be consumed liberally throughout the day - try for 4 to 6 eight-ounce glasses daily. Remember as well, that **juices** are mostly water, and most fruits and vegetables are 85% to 97% water. Thus, ample water is usually consumed while enjoying the fresh foods (salads, fruit bowls, etc.) contained in a vegan diet. However, a glass of **fruit juice, soy milk, nut milk, tea,** or **pure water**, as often as is convenient during the day, is a good idea during pregnancy.

Obtaining pure water is not so easy these days. If she must, the pregnant woman should buy purified or distilled drinking water, install an effective filtration device in her home, or otherwise assure the purity of her water supply.

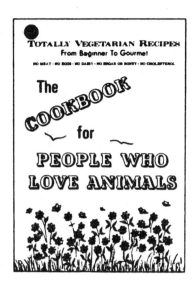

SO WHAT'S FOR DINNER?

Vegan cuisine is not only nutritious and tastes great, but is easy to prepare. After creating each dish once or twice, you will be able to prepare them in a short time. These foods, especially the grain dishes like burgers and lasagna, can be prepared ahead of time and refrigerated or frozen for future use. Salads and sandwiches can be made the night before and taken along to work or school to avoid the pitfalls of the cafeteria line. Leftovers of vegan meals last much longer in the refrigerator than do meat dishes, and will conveniently form the foundation for subsequent lunches, dinners and snacks. Even cleanup after preparing a vegan meal is more pleasant, without the remnants of animal flesh on the kitchen counter.

Following are sample menus for two days of delicious vegan meals, taken from the "Suggestion" list in Appendix 1. They are intentionally composed of dishes from the "Vegan Six": Grains and grain products, legumes, green and yellow vegetables, nuts and seeds, fruits, and "special foods", because of their high protein, vitamins, and mineral contents. Remember, these meal ideas are just suggested meal planning patterns; there are endless variations on these themes.

(Recipes for the following dishes, and many more, can be found in **THE COOKBOOK FOR PEOPLE WHO LOVE ANIMALS** - See Recommendations for Further Reading). Six more days of meal suggestions for pregnant women, adolescents, and children, are given in Appendix III.

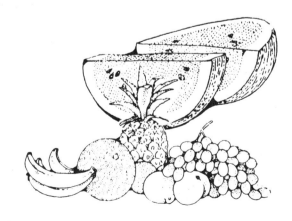

SAMPLE MENU

DAY ONE

BREAKFAST: 3/4 cup Whole Grain Cereal, (Rolled Oat Granola, Multi-grain Hot Cereal,etc.) Topped by Fruit, Chopped Almonds and Raisins, with 1/2 cup Soy Milk or Sunflower Milk made fresh in the blender;

PROTEIN: 8 g. CALCIUM: 100 mgs. IRON: 2 mgs.

LUNCH: Medium Green Salad -
    with fresh Carrots,
    1/4 cup Alfalfa Sprouts,
    Tahini Dressing
Tofu (4 oz.) Cutlet Sandwich -
    2 slices Whole Grain Bread
    "trimmings" of Lettuce, Tomatoes, Soy Mayonnaise

PROTEIN: 30 g. CALCIUM: 440 mgs. IRON: 10 mgs.

DINNER: Soup (1 cup) - Bean/Barley/Vegetable, etc.;
Garden Green Salad
    Italian Dressing;
Vegetable/Grain combination main dish (6 oz. serving)
    (with an added legume feature like Tofu, Lentils, Beans, Sprouts,
    Chickpeas, etc.);
      for example,

    Tofu/Millet Loaf w/Carrot, Onion, & Peppers,
       or
    Oriental-Style stir-fried Vegetables
      with Tofu and Cashews,
      over 1 cup Noodles or Rice;
Side dishes of 1cup steamed Broccoli and/or Carrots
    with Nutritional Yeast Gravy

PROTEIN: 32 g. CALCIUM: 460 mgs. IRON: 13 mgs.

SNACKS: 3/4 cup Almond and Raisin mix consumed during the day,
    plus any of the following, if desired:
Fruits,
Frozen Juice "Pops",
Fruit or Vegetable Juices,
Fruit Smoothies,
Vegan Baked Goods - Apple Pie, Banana Bread, etc.
Popcorn, etc.

PROTEIN 5 g. CALCIUM 200 mg. IRON 5 mg.

When thirsty, enjoy liberal amounts of pure water and fruit and vegetable juices.

DAY TWO

BREAKFAST: 4 Whole Wheat Pancakes (4" diameter)
topped with Maple Syrup and/or Fruit Spread (Apple Butter, Peach Compote, etc.)
4-ounce glass Soy Milk.
Fruit Juice,
Coffee substitute (Postum, Cafix, Pero, etc.), or Herbal Tea.

PROTEIN 18 gms. CALCIUM 180 mgs. IRON 2 mgs.

LUNCH: One bowl Tossed Salad
2 tablespoons Tahini Dressing;
One sandwich (2 slices Whole Wheat, Pumpernickel, Rye Bread, or
Whole Wheat Pita) with
1/2 cup Hummus (Chick Pea Spread),
Lettuce, Tomato,
1/4 cup Alfalfa Sprouts, Onion;
or
2 tablespoons Peanut Butter with Banana & Raisins
4-oz.glass Soy Milk (Edensoy, Ah Soy, etc.)

PROTEIN 27 gms. CALCIUM 400 mgs. IRON 10 mgs.

DINNER: Medium Garden Green Salad
Vinegar/Nutritional Yeast Dressing;
6 oz. Whole Wheat or Artichoke Spaghetti w/Tomato Sauce
(with Tofu, TVP and Mushrooms);
2 slices Whole Grain Bread with Garlic Spread;
or
One 8 oz. bowl Red-Bean Vegetarian Chili,
with tofu or T.V.P.
1 cup Steamed Collards and Yellow Squash,
topped with Tomato Sauce or Mushroom Gravy

PROTEIN 28 gms. CALCIUM 420 mgs. IRON 13 mgs.

SNACKS: 3/4 cup Almond and Raisin Mix and any of the following:
3 Peanut Butter/Oatmeal Cookies
4 oz. bowl Oat Granola and Soy Milk
Vegan baked goods
Garden green salads

PROTEIN 5 gms. CALCIUM 200 mgs. IRON5 mgs.

By the end of her day, the expectant mother (or anyone else) would have consumed:

more than 75 grams of (slowly absorbed, high quality vegetable) protein,

over 1200 milligrams of calcium,

and at least 30 milligrams of iron,

all of which meet the Recommended Daily Allowance for pregnant women.

As you can see, vegan nutrition is certainly no hardship for the tastebuds or the tummy!

NUTRITIONAL PRINCIPLES

Some good nutritional principles to keep in mind while preparing meals are as follows:

1. Emphasize fresh, raw foods (salads, fruit bowls, sprouts, etc.) over cooked foods. For children, one can puree or blend fresh fruits or vegetables in the blender or food processor, such as raw apples for applesauce instead of cooked.

2. Don't cook the life out of your food. Lightly steaming vegetables is recommended over frying or high temperature baking.

3. Avoid **excessive** amounts of cooking oils and oil-containing foods, as well as hydrogenated oils used in margarines and baked goods.

4. Starches (grains, potatoes, pastas, etc.) should be the main calorie (energy) source of your diet, and the center of at least one main meal each day. When entering the kitchen with the question, "What shall I make for dinner?," remember that this reliable "meal formula" for a high-protein, balanced dinner, is as simple as "one, two, three:"

1. GARDEN SALAD with dressing

2. MAIN DISH ENTREE
Grain and Legume Combination
("2 1/2 to 1" - Grain to Legume Ratio)
(e.g., 2 1/2 cups rice to 1 cup pinto beans)

3. SIDE DISHES
Green and Yellow Vegetables
(Lightly steamed, served with gravy)

In planning meals, remember salads and soups are good "first courses", and add interest and nutrition. They are also good vehicles for high-mineral sea vegetables such as kombu, arame, and nori (available at your health food store).

Very importantly, find out what foods your family likes the most (potato salad, pastas, etc.) and make them often. Become comfortable using seasonings and spices to make meals taste delicious.

The following foods, although not essential nutrients, are extremely useful ingredients in vegan cuisine: Whole grains, legumes, tahini (sesame seed butter), tofu, tamari sauce, and nutritional yeast, all available at the local health food store. Often, tahini can be purchased at a reasonable rate, in Armenian or Greek bakeries.

As well, these vegan "reliables" should probably be purchased in one of your early shopping trips: herbs for seasoning (oregano, basil, dill, turmeric, ginger, etc.), thickeners for gravies (arrowroot, oat flour, etc.), herbal teas for beverages, and carob for a chocolate substitute.

Find a good source for high quality produce and staples. Investigate your area. Locate the farmers' markets, health food stores, food co-ops, produce stands, and supermarket produce managers who can supply your needs for good vegetables and fruits at reasonable cost, with a minimum of chemical pollutants.

Taking a vegetarian cooking course, frequently offered at local colleges, adult education centers, YMCA's, etc., is a wise investment. Such a course will greatly increase familiarity with purchasing and preparing vegetarian ingredients. As well, such a course is a great place to meet other nutrition-minded people and to make new vegetarian friends.

GRAIN IDEAS

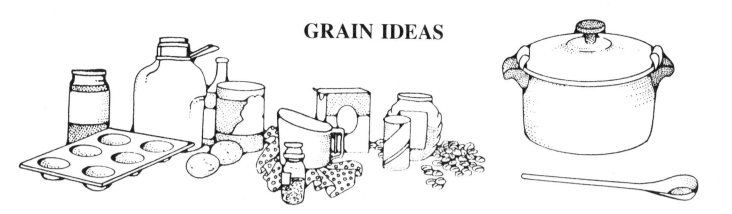

In planning vegan meals, and when faced with a pantry full of raw ingredients, some basic principles are of value. Grains and grain products should form the centerpiece of most dinners or luncheon meals. The vegan chef should be comfortable in working with grains, as they are nutritious, inexpensive, filling, and easy to prepare. Rice, barley, millet, or quinoa, can be used in soups, vegetable bakes, or grainburgers. They are a reliable, high-protein complement to vegetables and legumes.

For most grains, the basic recipe for preparation is approximately two parts water to one part grain. Bring water to a boil, add grain, cover and simmer on low heat, until the water is absorbed. When grain is done, remove from heat, uncover pot, and allow to cool without stirring. A rice cooker, available at Oriental groceries, will make perfect rice and other grains every time, with a quart of water and a touch of a button.

The variations that follow will add interest and flavor to any grain dish. These ideas will work equally well with whole grain brown rice, millet, bulghur, barley, quinoa, cous cous, etc.

a) Add some nuts (walnuts, pecans, a few peanuts, etc.) to the cooking water, and cook the grain with the nuts. Optionally, you can add a few more just before serving.

b) Add some seeds - sunflower, sesame, caraway, pumpkin. You can roast the seeds lightly in the oven before adding them to the cooking water of the grain. Adds an interesting texture and flavor.

c) Cook the grain with vegetables - chop up some onions, corn, celery, chunked squash, or root vegetables like carrots, parsnips, etc.

(d) Add some herbs and spices to the cooking water - tamari, miso, Bronner's Vegetable Boullion, Quick-Sip, or classic spices like sage, basil, and oregano.

e) Use combinations of grains - for example, mix rice with barley, millet, rye, bulghur, or oat flakes, etc.

f) Add cooked legumes to the grain - soak some beans overnight, spill off the soaking water in the morning, cook, and add to the grain before serving.

g) Grains can be roasted lightly in the oven before cooking for a firmer texture and a "nut-like" flavor.

h) Serve with a gravy. Here's some ideas:

Use a starch-based body for the gravy; i.e., a little arrowroot, tamari, water, and parsley flakes.

Oat flour, lightly browned in a pan with tamari,
water and spices, makes a good gravy base.

Tomato-based sauces and miso-type stocks are vegan classics, as are those based upon tahini or nutritional yeast.

i) Increase the important trace mineral content of the diet by sprinkling powdered kelp on grains, salads, and side dishes; learn to cook with "sea vegetables"; i.e., arame, dulse, or kombu (a potato-textured stalk), added to rice, soups, or salads.

j) Adding a small amount of olive or safflower oil to the grain cooking water, helps prevent the grains from sticking together.

Though not actually grains, here are a few kind thoughts about their "protein cousins," beans and legumes.

USING BEANS FOR HUMAN BEINGS

Nutritionists have long recognized the nutritional bonanza that is offered by the family of legumes. Beans and their relatives offer superb protein quality, equal or superior to that found in meats, while being far less expensive and free of animal fat. Legumes are making a triumphant return to meal plans everywhere.

a) To use them most effectively, beans should be soaked overnight in a covered bowl, or non-aluminum pot, to prepare them for use in tomorrow's soup, chili, or casserole. A container of soaking beans should be a regular fixture on the kitchen counter.

The overnight soaking of the beans, followed by spilling off the soaking water, will soften the beans' starches, activate important enzymes, and minimize problems with intestinal gas, experienced by some people who eat legumes. The decanted water will carry away a bean sugar called hemicellulose, a main culprit in gas formation. The beans should then be fully cooked and used in your favorite recipes.

b) Beans should be added to soups and grain dishes, and can be mashed into a pâté, mixed with tamari, miso, onions, or garlic, and served on taco shells, pita bread, or crackers.

c) Don't forget the other excellent members of the "legume clan", peas, split peas, lentils, chick peas (garbanzos), and alfalfa sprouts. Add peas to soups, or serve as side dishes (peas for optimism!); soak lentils overnight (or until soft) and add to salads, combine with vegetables in loaves, or make lentil stew (dal) to serve with rice, vegetables and bread; soak and cook (or sprout) garbanzo beans, mash, then add olive oil and seasoning to create "hummus" - delicious spread on bread.

d) Remember, all legumes can be sprouted! This activates their enzymes; partially dismantling their starches. Sprouting is a highly recommended maneuver that will increase the nutritional value and digestibility of all legumes.

e) Learn to prepare and enjoy whole beans rather than refined legume products like tofu, TVP, etc. Tofu is a processed food, lacking the "germ" and other nutrients of the whole bean, and is far more expensive.

f) However, tofu fans can still enjoy this excellent food - one can use tofu in many vegan recipes and it is a convenient and versatile form of legume protein. Tofu is also an excellent "transition" food for those evolving past meat-eating, yet desiring a "chewy" protein source. Tofu's bland taste merely signifies that it is an ingredient; it acquires the taste of any sauce or seasoning with which it is mixed.

Tofu can be blended with fruit to make tofu "yogurt"; mashed with tahini, tamari, and turmeric to create tofu "omelettes"; cubed, marinated and stir-fried in vegetable sautes; blended into gravies; used as a binder in cake batters and casseroles; mashed and seasoned for a sandwich spread; sliced and sauteed as "cutlets"; and in many other delicious and imaginative ways, such as "sour cream" and "cream cheese", that will replace dairy products in the diet.

Tofu can be purchased at any supermarket in the produce section, and especially good tofu can be purchased at Oriental food stores. Buy the tofu with the most distant date stamped on the package, and at home, open the package, spill out the water, and store the tofu in a closed container in the refrigerator, covered with fresh water. Change the water daily. Each block of tofu should not remain in your refrigerator for very long - it should be used and enjoyed!

CLINICAL NOTES

In my experience, women eating in a vegan style throughout their pregnancies have easier labors and deliveries, as they are generally healthier women, and their babies are not excessively large.

Of importance to many, is that vegan women are often left with fewer "stretch marks" on their abdomen, perhaps due to their leaner and more resilient skin. A generous amount of avocados and nut butters in the diet, an occasional teaspoon of food-grade linseed oil on bread, and weekly applications of olive oil to the abdominal skin, are reported to help the skin accommodate stretch without forming "striae".

The needs for some nutrients may change during the course of pregnancy. A high-carbohydrate diet is essential throughout pregnancy, and is an aid to preventing morning sickness.

As mentioned, the amount of protein-containing foods should be increased in the final three months (more tofu, greens, legumes, etc.) to help protect against preeclampsia (toxemia of pregnancy).

The body sends many messages during pregnancy, expressing its needs for certain foods, as well as for exercise, and emotional support. These messages should be listened to, and fulfilled in a healthy manner. A woman may indulge "craving" for any vegan food, and she may find she has a special desire for those foods containing "earth minerals", like iron, zinc, and selenium. Mushrooms, yeast, and root vegetables, contain these minerals, and should be enjoyed regularly.

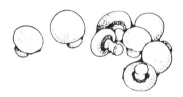

AN OUNCE OF PREVENTION

Especially during pregnancy, it is important to guard against avoidable hazards in the environment. Toxic, volatile chemicals lurk in nail polish removers, spot removers, paint thinners, lacquers, varnish, and arts and crafts materials. Avoid skin contact with pesticides, and anti-dandruff shampoos containing zinc pyridine-thione.

Lead in tap water (from lead pipes) can interfere with brain formation in the developing fetus[87]. Consider having your water tested, and changing to bottled drinking water, if necessary.

Lead can also leach into food from cans, making refrigerator storage in plastic containers a wise maneuver. Of course, fresh or frozen foods are far preferable to canned goods, and do not pose the risk of lead contamination.

Two **avoidable toxins**, dangerous to both mother and fetus, are **alcohol**[88] and **cigarette smoke**[89]. Pregnancy is an excellent time to evolve past these two detrimental habits.

An expectant mother should do all she can to become physically strong and balanced for her approaching labor: a daily walk in the sunshine for strength, stretching exercises for flexibility, and plenty of laughter for happiness, are also vital ingredients in the recipe for good health. Attending prenatal classes to learn about the process of pregnancy and labor is also a key to a successful birth day for mother, child, and the rest of the family.

Most women find that their pregnancies are a time of health, with great feelings of well being. The pregnant vegan woman should be confident about her diet and lifestyle, and look forward to the delivery of her baby and to nursing her healthy child.

Chapter 3

THE VEGAN DIET FOR NURSING MOTHERS

SOREN WAGNER at 6 weeks.

Breastfeeding is certainly the best, most natural form of nutrition during the infant's first year of life, and holds great benefits for the mother as well. All the child's nutritional needs through the first six months can be met through the miraculous infant food that is human mother's breastmilk.

The breastmilk of vegan mothers is fully nutritious for infants, and contains the full complement of energy, protein, and vitamins, needed for the rapid growth of life's first half year. Breastmilk not only contains nutrients, but also antibodies that bolster the baby's immune system. Very importantly, the breastfeeding years create emotional security in the child through the many hours of intimate contact with the mother.

The breastmilk of vegan mothers also provides a measure of safety for the baby. Nursing women who eat the conventional animal-based American diet, consume meat, dairy products, and fish that contain chemical contaminants, such as hormones, antibiotics, and pesticides. These substances are then secreted into the woman's breastmilk.[18]

During its first year, the baby is still developing its brain, endocrine glands, and other vital tissues - and thus is vulnerable to even small amounts of these potent chemicals. Vegan women, who do not eat animal products, secrete far less of these contaminants into their breastmilk than flesh and dairy-eating women[90]. Thus, vegan infants are spared a potentially serious chemical assault early in life.

Breastfeeding also provides many benefits for the mother. The baby's nursing stimulates hormone release from her pituitary gland that helps the uterus return to its non-pregnant size. Breastfeeding also helps the mother "burn off" excess fatty tissue she may have accumulated during pregnancy. Of course, the emotional bonding that develops between mother and child through breastfeeding helps create a lifetime bridge of love and trust.

Worldwide, there is a healthy resurgence in breastfeeding, and it should be encouraged throughout North America. Pregnant women are encouraged to contact their local chapter of **La Leche League International** for further information. Their central office address is 9616 Minneapolis Boulevard, Franklin Park, IL 60131-8209. Excellent books, with many helpful suggestions on breastfeeding, available through La Leche League, include Karen Pryor's **Nursing Your Baby** and **The Womanly Art of Breastfeeding.**

It is important for the breastfeeding mother to properly care for her nipples to prevent cracking of the skin. A few weeks before delivery, massaging wheat germ oil or cocoa butter into the nipples and surrounding areola, will help prevent soreness. Gently massaging the nipples with a washcloth-wrapped finger several times daily will prepare the tissues for baby's nursing. Air baths and moderate sun baths also promote skin health for the breasts (and for the rest of the body).

To minimize stress upon the nipple tissues during nursing, alternate breasts every five minutes, and be sure the baby takes enough of the nipple and areola into its mouth while nursing. A nursing session should end by the mother inserting a finger into the corner of the baby's mouth, and pulling away the lip from the nipple, thus breaking the baby's suction hold upon the breast.

If a mother is unable or does not desire to breastfeed, a commercial soy-based formula should be offered through bottle feeding (see Chapter 4 and Appendix V - "Dairy Alternatives").

Although soy-based formulas should be the infant's dietary staple, other beverages can be used to supplement a breastfeeding program. These include the liquid from inside a fresh coconut, or lukewarm, distilled water, sweetened by soaking two or three dates in a glass for an hour. (See Appendix V)

It is very important to position the baby properly while feeding from breast or bottle. The nasal cavity and the mouth both share a common passage at the back of the throat. When the baby is lying on its back, and fluids are swallowed, the liquid can be forced up into the back of the nasal cavity.

NEVER LET YOUR BABY NURSE FROM THE BREAST OR A BOTTLE WHILE LYING FLAT ON HIS/HER BACK!

Such a supine position will permit the back of the nose, including the openings into the canals leading to the middle ear, to fill with milk, fruit juice, or other liquid. This subtle, but important, mechanism is one of the greatest sources of recurring middle ear infections and chronic nasal discharges and allergies in children.

The mother using the nursing bottle (with a collapsable inner liner) instead of the breast, should have the same awareness of proper positioning of the baby. The liquid in the bottle is meant to go into the baby's stomach only, not up into the nose or ears!

Always make sure the baby's upper body is well supported while nursing. The line of the baby's trunk and head, while being held in its mother's arms, should create a 40 to 60-degree angle with the floor. (See the photograph of vegan mother, Victoria Moran, holding her daughter, Rachael, in the correct feeding position.)

The nursing bottle must be held in the mother's hand, not propped against the baby's face. The pressure from a bottle leaning against the baby's mouth can deform the growing jaw and teeth.

The nipple and bottle should be washed and dried after each feeding. Be sure that the hole in the nipple is large enough so that the baby does not have to suck excessively hard, which can lead to stomach distension. Using a pin, enlarge the nipple hole so the milk drips easily from the bottle when inverted.

Try to keep a nursing or "vegetable milk" bottle feeding as a separate meal from juice or other liquid feeding. Combining milk with juices can produce digestive problems for the baby. Avoid overfeeding, because too much of any liquid (soy milk, juice, etc.) can suppress the baby's desire to nurse. A decrease in the baby's nursing will eventually create a lessening in the mother's milk supply. (See "Juicy News").

TAKING CARE OF BABY'S TEETH

IMPORTANT - As the baby's teeth erupt, bottle feeding can pose a hazard to tooth health. Any sweet liquid, including breast milk, soy milk, and fruit juices, when left in a child's mouth, will be fermented to acids and can cause serious tooth decay.

DO NOT LEAVE A BOTTLE IN THE CRIB FOR THE CHILD TO NURSE FROM DURING THE NIGHT (ESPECIALLY FILLED WITH FRUIT JUICE, MILK, FORMULA, OR OTHER SWEET LIQUIDS), AS THIS WILL DESTROY THE TEETH (AS WELL AS LEAD TO EAR AND CHEST INFECTIONS!)

If the child needs the bottle for his/her "security", then make it a bottle filled with water.

The dietary guidelines presented for the pregnant woman will also meet the nutritional needs for the nursing mother. Iron and calcium-rich foods - see Appendix I - (with supplementation, if necessary) - should be continued well into, and beyond lactation, as the mother's iron stores may have been taxed during pregnancy. A blood count at two weeks, and again at six weeks after delivery should be done to evaluate the need for continuation of supplements.

VITAMINS B-6, B-12, and VITAMIN D

As always, fresh fruits and vegetables are the major and best source of vitamins for human beings. The nursing mother should enjoy fresh salads and steamed vegetables throughout lactation.

IMPORTANT NOTICE for NURSING MOTHERS ABOUT VITAMIN B-12

Not only is the mother's health dependent upon an adequate vitamin supply, but the nursing infant's sole source of vitaminB-12 and other essential vitamins, comes from the milk made from the mother's blood. Thus, the nursing mother must be sure she has an adequate daily supply of these vitamins.

Vitamin B-12 that the nursing mother has stored in her own liver and muscles for her own use is not freely available to be secreted into the breastmilk for the infant. THUS, NURSING MOTHERS SHOULD BE SURE THEY CONSUME 3 TO 5 MICROGRAMS OF VITAMIN B-12 DAILY, USING B-12 FORTIFIED FOODS, OR SUPPLEMENT TABLETS IF NECESSARY TO ASSURE AN ADEQUATE B-12 SUPPLY FOR THE NURSING INFANT. (See "Vitamin B-12" in "Pregnancy" section).

Vitamin D is similarly essential for the mother's diet in order to provide it in ample amounts in the breastmilk for the baby. If ample amounts of sunshine are not freely available to the mother and infant, supplemental vitamin D should be taken.

Multivitamin supplements taken during pregancy should be continued through lactation to insure adequate daily vitamin supplies of at least three micrograms of B-12 and 400 I.U. of vitamin D - be sure to read the vitamin bottle label.

Beware of excessive vitamin B-6. This vitamin should be amply supplied through food sources, but caution is advised if the mother is taking supplemental vitamin B-6 for any reason. Doses of over 100 milligrams per day can suppress lactation and cause nerve injury.

WATER

The nursing mother should drink generous amounts of pure water and fruit and vegetable juices (try for six to eight 8-ounce glasses per day) to assure a bountiful supply of breast milk.

LIFESTYLE BALANCE

The months of breastfeeding should be a time when the woman becomes physically stronger. A brisk walk out in the sunshine every day, as well as a stretching and muscle-strengthening program, will make her better able to enjoy her daily work, nurse her baby well, and complete any healing necessary following the birth.

How babies and children are handled is a powerful shaper of their nervous systems and personalities. Because breast or bottle feeding is a time of intimate contact, the mother should take responsiblity to make each feeding as pleasant as possible. The atmosphere and the mother's emotional state while nursing should be calm and supportive. The presence of loving family members, of other breastfeeding mothers, or gentle background music (classical, easy listening, etc.) greatly enriches the nursing experience, as does nursing (discreetly) out-of-doors, in a peaceful, natural setting.

Many women report that nursing is one of the most fulfilling times of their lives. The nursing mother should learn all she can about breastfeeding so she can become skillful, confident, and relaxed while nurturing her infant child. She should be assured that the vegan diet that sustained her and her baby during pregnancy will provide full and balanced nourishment throughout the months of breastfeeding.

The child will usually announce (through nipple-chewing and other signs) that he or she is ready for weaning to a cup. This usually happens by age nine through twenty-four months, but if at all possible, let the child decide. There is no hurry to halt breastfeeding, and the experience of nursing a child is a precious one, not to be rushed.

Lifelong vegan, film actress, SUMMER PHOENIX, at 8 years old.

Chapter 4

THE VEGAN DIET FOR CHILDREN

---

*If you are already a parent, not expecting a child, you may be reading **PREGNANCY, CHILDREN, and THE VEGAN DIET**, to learn what to feed your children, and thus, starting your reading here. It is strongly suggested that you first read Chapter 2 (Vegan Nutrition During Pregnancy) to become familiar with the principles of vegan nutrition that will be used in this chapter to plan meals for children.

Throughout the world, children are growing into healthy, full-size adults without eating animal products[91]. The question is not, **can** a child be raised healthily on a vegan diet, but how to do it properly. In this chapter, we will consider how to create a balanced vegan diet for infants and growing children.

The times seem appropriate to reconsider what foods we are feeding to our children. American children are now showing three worrisome health traits, related to their fat-laden diet, that concern pediatricians and public health authorities.

The average child in the United States:

1. **Is too fat**.
a) 60% of all American children are obese. (Over 30% of their body weight is fat).
b) 90% of American children cannot pass a rudimentary physical fitness test (such as performing one chin-up).

2. **Reaches puberty too early** - Since World War II, the age of onset of menstruation of American girls has fallen from the average of sixteen years to eleven. There has been a corresponding increase in the incidence of breast cancer in young women[92].

3. **Suffers from serious, diet-implicated diseases**, that range from the troublesome, like allergies and eczema, to the debilitating, like juvenile arthritis and asthma, to the fatal, such as leukemia and strokes. (Yes, strokes. Each year, over 1,000 American teenagers suffer devastating strokes from high blood pressure and arteries clogged with fat).

Let's examine the role of meat and dairy products in the diet of the American child and see why it is time for a change.

Vegan mother and daughter, VICTORIA MORAN and RACHAEL.

North American children are usually fed large amounts of meat, poultry, fish, milk, and dairy products, under the assumption that the high protein and/or calcium content of these products is "good for growing children." Medical evidence is now suggesting that the opposite may be the case; that the present meat-heavy American diet is actually undermining our children's good health.[26-28]

Meats of all kinds, especially beef, pork, and the prepared meats found in fast foods like cheeseburgers, hot dogs, sausage, pizza, etc., are laden with animal fat. As previously cited, eating animal fats has been strongly linked to clogging arteries in children as young as 9 months old[94]! The almost constant flood of fat flowing through our children's bloodstreams from their unbalanced diet, forms the foundation for heart attacks and strokes, as adults, and sometimes in childhood[95]. High fat levels are also incriminated in fostering some forms of cancer, in breast and prostate gland[96].

As previously described, a high-fat diet also promotes higher levels of sex and growth hormones that circulate in the body[97]. The effects of these higher hormone levels are of great concern, as growth and maturation are crowded into disturbingly early years.

The famous "growth spurt" of American children is being questioned by pediatricians and other health professionals as being something other than a sign of healthy maturation[98]. Could it be a result of the excessive fat, protein and added sex and growth hormones found in meat and dairy products which American youths consume in such volume? There is a strong correlation between meat and dairy consumption and an early and rapid growth spurt (including early onset of menses in girls), and the subsequent development of breast cancers and other malignancies[99].

As noted by John Scharffenberg, M. D., M.P.H., medical nutritionist and Associate Professor of Applied Nutrition, Loma Linda University:

"The average, so-called 'normal' child matures too rapidly here in the United States . . . it is known that vegetarian children mature later, begin menstruating later in life, have a delayed growth spurt, but do end up as tall as others, and their adult teeth emerge later in their childhood.

Is this delay in maturation to be recommended? Consider these facts. It is known that women with menarche (age of first menstruation) before age 13 have 4.2 times the risk of breast cancer than those women whose menarche occurs after age 17, according to Dr. T. Hirayama in a study of 142,000 Japanese women. The "normal" fat, early to grow, early to die, American standard is not to be recommended. A diet which delays premature growth, which decreases heart attacks (the pathogenesis of which begins in infancy), and which decreases cancer mortality, is to be recommended."

Lifelong vegan, TAHIRA McCORMACK, at 16 months.

An additional health hazard lurking in meat and dairy products was revealed by a huge "nutrition disaster" in Puerto Rico in 1985. In that country, hundreds of boys and girls, age two through adolescence, suddenly developed breasts and pubic hair, and the very young girls began to menstruate. After careful investigation, the evidence incriminated the milk from cows, and the meat of chickens that were fed the sex hormone, **stilbesterol**, to fatten them and increase milk production.[100]

The female children are at risk for developing tumors in their breasts, and cysts on their ovaries, thus becoming destined for eventual surgery. The effects on the boys of such early exposure to potent female hormones is not yet known, but is quite worrisome.

In the United States, powerful growth and sex hormones are fed to farm animals[101], and may play a role in some of the early pubertal changes seen among our youth. Fortunately, vegan children have no worries of hidden hormone augmentation in their food.

THEY GROW UP BIG AND STRONG...

Some nutritionists have expressed concern that vegan children may not receive all the calories and protein they require, especially before age two, and thus may be at risk for growth retardation. The theory is that the high fiber content of the vegan diet, while a boon to adults in lowering cholesterol and banishing obesity, may be a hindrance to the normal growth of children.

The concern is that if a child fills his or her small stomach with non-absorbable cellulose (fiber), from whole grains, greens, and fibrous fruits, the child may be unable to consume sufficient calories and protein. It has also been postulated that the fiber may carry vital nutrients out of the intestine before they are absorbed.

The focus upon excessive fiber loads may be valid, as children do require ample amounts of energy and vitamins in readily available form. However, there are dietary strategies to reduce fiber loads and optimize nutrient delivery by using "nutrient-dense" foods and other techniques. See "Juicy News," and "Introducing Solid Foods," for further descriptions of these strategies.

Inadequate nutrition does not seem to be a major problem for most vegan childen. Medical studies have shown vegan children grow to be as tall and strong as their meat-eating peers[102].

A flesh-free diet has also been shown to support healthy **intellectual** growth, as IQ tests show that children raised as vegans develop equal or higher intelligence than their meat and dairy-eating peers[30b].

Although vegan children do seem to be leaner then their omnivorous classmates, there is no cause for worry. The greatest determinant of the child's size is the genetic inheritance they receive from their parents. Many "small" children are just normal children of shorter parents, who happen to be vegan. Tall vegan parents have tall vegan children. Time and good nutrition permit children to attain the full potential of their genetic heritage.

Needed nutritional research on vegetarians should include establishing normal growth curves for vegan children. Much confusion among parents and health professionals would thus be allayed.

Again, a balanced vegan diet, with reduced fiber content, and rich in the protein and calorie-containing "All-Stars" from the "Vegan Six", with supplemental vitamin and mineral "insurance" as discussed, should provide optimal growth for any child.

Let's now re-examine one class of foods in the current American style of nutrition that, though promoted as a "Basic Food Group", may actually be a major source of health problems for our children.

Hollywood screen star, vegan, RIVER PHOENIX, age 17.

BE WARY OF DAIRY!

To many mothers, it seems natural to give children cow's milk to drink, and dairy products, like cheese and ice cream, to eat. However, clinical experience suggests that cow's milk is not a natural food for human children (or adults!) and actually is linked to many of the health problems (runny noses, allergies, ear infections, recurrent bronchitis, etc.) that bring people to the doctor's office.[104] Let's look at the realities of cow's milk (and products made from it) and see why it is fit food only for calves.

MILK

Standard whole milk is **over 90% water**, with **3% butterfat**, and **2% protein**. It is made for turning a 45-pound calf into a 300-pound cow in a year, and is marvelously designed to accomplish this task. Its content of **sodium, fat**, and **phosporous**, is much higher than that of human breast milk, while its potassium supply is lower.

The protein in cow's milk is mostly **casein**, which forms hard curds in the stomach of infants. Conversely, the predominant protein in human milk is **lactalbumin**, which is far more easily digestible by babies.

These contrasts are as they should be. Cows are faster growing, much larger than people, and genetically distant from humans. Nature has designed the milk of each animal species specifically to meet the nutritional needs for the young of that species.

People are the only animals that drink the milk of the mother of another species. Most animals stop drinking milk altogether after weaning. Just as it is unnatural for a dog to nurse from a giraffe, a child drinking the milk of a mother cow is just as strange, yet it is an image that has been made as "wholesome as apple pie" through modern advertising. It is not surprising that problems ensue from this inherently unnatural act...

Five substances have been found in many dairy products that can create imbalance and disease within the human body:

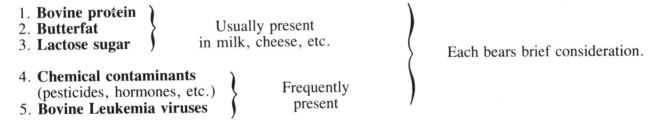

1. **Bovine protein**
2. **Butterfat**   } Usually present
3. **Lactose sugar**   in milk, cheese, etc.

} Each bears brief consideration.

4. **Chemical contaminants**
   (pesticides, hormones, etc.) } Frequently
5. **Bovine Leukemia viruses**   present

With each swallow of a milkshake, or mouthful of cheese or ice cream, bovine protein is smeared upon the child's throat membranes, tonsils, adenoids, and other gateways into the immune system. Fragments of milk protein can cross the surface membranes[104], and when the protein of another animal is introduced into one's immune system, an allergic/immune response is created in many places in the body[105].

A common reaction to such an assault by a foreign protein in our immune system is an outpouring of mucus from the nasal and throat membranes, upon which the invading substance is applied. The resulting mucus flow can create the chronic runny noses, persistent sore throats, hoarseness, bronchitis, and the recurrent ear infections that plague so many children[106] (and their parents).

Other body membranes, such as those lining the lungs and joints, can react to dairy protein and become swollen and inflamed, contributing to the conditions of asthma and rheumatoid arthritis. Patients with asthma[107] and rheumatoid arthritis[108] have been shown to improve dramatically when dairy protein is removed from the diet.

These common childhood afflictions, and other low-grade allergic-type problems, like eczema and psoriasis, often prove to be reactions to various animal proteins in sensitive children. They can clear completely when dairy products are deleted from the diet[109]. Some breastfeeding babies even react with these symptoms when the nursing mother herself consumes dairy products.

Low-fat milk is little better than whole milk, as it still contains 1% butterfat, and a full complement of allergy-inciting milk protein. Be aware also that "calcium caseinate" and "whey powder" - waste from the cheese-making process - are both derived from milk protein, and are common allergy-inciting dairy components used in breads, pastry, and commercial baked goods. **The wise shopper is a reader of labels**, and should be aware of all the ingredients in the products purchased to avoid hidden dairy substances.

The **butterfat** (cream) in milk and dairy products can contribute to the **clogging of arteries** of children[112], is one of the chief culprits in the tragedy of childhood obesity[113], and can also contribute to the elevated hormone levels that may foster the growth of cancers[114].

It is important as well to understand the true nature of dairy products, which are so heavily advertised as wholesome, nutritious food. At the dairy, the 3% butterfat in whole milk is concentrated to 15% - 40%, and then processed so people will buy it and eat it. This highly concentrated animal fat is:

(a) mixed with **sugar**, frozen, and sold as **ice cream**,
(b) congealed with **mold** into **cheese**,
(c) churned with **air** into **butter**,
(d) mixed with **sugar and cocoa** to be sold as **milk chocolate**,
(e) fermented with **bacteria** into sour cream and yogurt.

These are all forms of the same artery-clogging, cancer-promoting butterfat.

The butterfat is not the only dairy threat to the health of our children. The sugar in milk, lactose, requires an enzyme, **lactase**, for digestion. Twenty percent of Caucasian children and eighty percent of Black children do not have the lactase enzyme in the instestinal wall to digest lactose. These children suffer severe abdominal cramps, diarrhea, and dehydration when they drink cow's milk, yet most do exceedingly well on milk made from soy protein. This would seem to be another powerful argument for leaving cow's milk to the calves.

Cow's milk also contains the accumulated **pesticides** that have been sprayed on the grains fed to the cattle[110], as well as the female **hormones** (estrogens, etc.) given to the cow to increase her milk production and body fat[111].

Another ominous reason to avoid feeding milk products to children is that an estimated **20% of milk-producing cows** in America are infected with **leukemia** viruses[115]. The infected cow pours these cancer-causing viruses out in her milk[116], which is then pooled with **all** the milk in the tanker truck on the way to the dairy. These cancer-inducing viruses are resistant to killing by pasteurization, and have been recovered from supermarket milk supplies[117]. Is it a coincidence that the highest rates of leukemia are found in children ages 3 through 13, who consume the most milk and dairy products[118]? It may also come as no surprise that the occupational group with the highest rate of leukemia is dairy farmers[118a]! These people not only drink cow's milk, but they splash it on their hands and breathe the air of the dairy barn for prolonged periods.

Human children have no nutritional requirements for cow's milk, and grow up healthy and strong without it. Ample calcium and protein for growing children can be obtained from plant sources exclusively. Mothers who do not give milk or dairy products to their children should feel that they are helping their children stay healthy, rather than depriving them.

Fortunately, there are delicious substitutes for all dairy products, (pre-packaged soy milks, non-dairy ice creams and yogurts, etc.), and children may be introduced to these early in life. Check with the people at your local health food store for non-dairy products, and see the many dairy substitutes and treat recipes in pure vegetarian cookbooks.

When thirsty, children can drink pure water, fruit juices, or vegetable juices. Carrot juice is an especially sweet favorite among kids. Nut milks, made in the blender with water, using almonds, cashews, sunflower seeds, or nut butters, (with tofu and/or tahini added for extra protein and calcium) soon become preferred dairy replacements.

Both parents and children will enjoy the non-dairy alternatives, listed in Appendix V, for pouring on their breakfast cereal, for beverage use, and for desserts.

Fortunately, as children are weaned from dairy products, they seem to automatically increase their desire for greens, nuts, nut butters, and other calcium-containing foods. The mother should be aware of this tendency and become familiar with various ways of preparing these foods, using gravies or other sauces to enhance tastes and textures of these calcium sources.

Thus, cow's milk (and subsequently all the products made from it), although portrayed to the public as healthful food, is actually a white fluid laced with fat and foreign animal protein, and not infrequently containing leukemia viruses, chemical contaminants, pesticides and/or sex hormones. In view of the many safer, more nutritious alternatives, parents should feel good about freeing themselves and their children from the milk and dairy foods in their diets.

Vegan child ROSE PEDEN at 2 3/4, with friend.

Let's look at some of the specific nutritional needs of children, and see why the vegan diet, completely free of animal products, works so well for them. The U. S. Recommended Daily Allowances for protein, calcium and iron for children are listed below:

AGE (years)	WEIGHT (pounds)	PROTEIN (gms/day)	CALCIUM (mgs/day)	IRON (mgs/day)
0 - 6 mos.	13	15	360	10
6 mos.- 1	20	20	540	15
1 - 3	29	23	800	15
4 - 6	44	30	800	10
7 - 10	62	34	800	10
11 - 14	99	45	1200	18
15 - 18	145	56	1200	18

Here's how a vegan diet can meet all of these nutritional needs.

Throughout the first eighteen months of life, especially as solid foods are introduced, the baby will be continuing to nurse on breastmilk or vitamin-fortified soy formula. Thus, she/he is furnished "nutritional insurance" while learning to enjoy the new, "more solid" world of vegan cuisine.

If breastfeeding is not desired or possible, a **soy-based** formula with liquid vitamin supplements, available through the pharmacy, should be given. Seek nutritional consultation from your physician or nutritionist. Soy beverages such as Edensoy and Ah Soy!, although nutritious and tasty drinks, should **not** be used as infant formula! (See Appendix V for dairy alternatives).

The baby should be weighed on an accurate scale at least once a week to provide reassurance of normal growth.

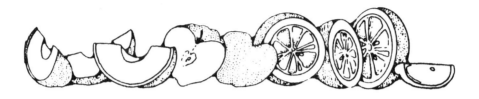

JUICY NEWS

Providing **water, glucose/energy, vitamins,** and **minerals,** pure fruit and vegetable juices can serve as "fiber-free" nutrition allies for the growing infant.

Juices should be offered at the age of two to three months, with watermelon, cantelope, or other melon being favorite "introduction" juices. Melons should be cleaned of seeds, chunked, liquified in the blender, and then strained through a cheesecloth or diaper. Older children do not need to have their juice or milk strained in this way, but such straining will protect an infant against choking on small pieces.

Juices, introduced in tiny quantities (1/4 teaspoon) at first, are gradually increased to four-ounce feedings by six months. To avoid interference with nursing, juice feedings should be given at least one hour before breastfeeding, or 2 1/2 to 3 hours after.

A variety of fruits and vegetables should be utilized to avoid monotony, mineral imbalances and allergic sensitization to particular vegetables. If the stools get loose, the juices may be too concentrated; dilute them with water.

Beware of feeding large volumes of juices that will decrease the baby's desire to nurse, and eventually, the mother's milk supply.

After one or two fruit juices are tolerated, vegetable juices should be introduced. Carrot juice with a small amount of celery juice is a favorite.

A recipe for a high vitamin C sweet drink is given by Freya Dinshah, as one of many valuable ideas presented in her excellent article, "Feeding Vegan Babies," published in "Ahimsa," Jan/March 1982, American Vegan Society, Malaga, New Jersey 08328. Freya suggests soaking overnight one teabag or teaspoon of loose rose hip tea and three dates. Strain the water the next morning and serve to baby. Juice from soaked raisins, figs, apricots, or other dried fruits, also please infants. Grape and apple juices can be introduced later.

READY, SET, GO...

Your baby will let you know when it is time to add solid foods. Around 5 to 6 months, the baby will start to show that it is not content with breastmilk alone. Crying after breastfeeding and nipple chewing are the child's ways of conveying its message that it is time for solid foods. But remember, too early an introduction of solid foods decreases the child's desire to nurse, and increases the chance of the baby developing food allergies. Of course, breastfeeding should continue throughout the time of introduction of solid foods.

The subject of how to introduce solid foods to an infant is surrounded by much lore and many opinions. Before considering specifics of what to feed and when, parents should realize they can make the entire process much easier on themselves and their baby:

First, relax. Throughout these "maiden voyages" into the world of solid foods, the child is still "protected" by a steady stream of nutritious breastmilk or soy infant formula. There is no danger of malnutrition if these life-sustaining liquids are freely available to the infant. This "coverage" creates a margin of safety for the child and the parents, who can then be assured that the child will not be deprived of adequate energy (calories) and vitamins while learning about foods that need chewing.

Secondly, realize that the "Food Introduction Guide" that follows, is simply what it says - a guide. It is a sequence of food introduction that has proven sucessful in many vegan families. **It is not the <u>only</u> sequence that works, and your baby will probably improvise his/her own.**

The parents should not feel anxious if the child is not eating a certain food in the "Guide" by a specified date. Nature has supplied infants with a marvelous ability to make food choices by color, texture, smell and taste, and thus to create a varied, fully nutritious diet for themselves. Let your child decide which foods interest them the most - and have several choices available on the plate for the child to point to. Every child is unique.

The gentlest, most effective role for the parent is that of helpful facilitator for the infant, as they both learn about each food. Let the baby handle the foods, smell them, rub it on their cheek - it's OK. Their world expands in wondrous ways.

Prefer to enjoy your baby's exploration with them, rather than creating the joyless "shoveling ritual" of "feeding the baby". Tune in to this magical process. Your child only passes though this chapter once. The vegan foods presented in the "Guide", with a "background" of breastmilk or soy formula, will allow plenty of time for the child to learn about foods he must choose, and chew!

Don't worry. With a variety of appropriate vegan whole foods available on the plate as suggested, Mother Nature will guide you and your child into the proper food choices. Don't be concerned if at a given feeding the baby concentrates upon one food or another. That food may well have a nutrient that their body senses it requires at that time. Let your child lead the way. Relax, and appreciate the magic of the process.

THE SOLID FOOD PARADE

1) Start with **fruits** - mashed banana is a classic "first food", followed by cooked peaches, applesauce, fruit compote, etc. Banana causes few allergic reactions, has a smooth consistency, and contains more food value than cereals. Begin with a small amount mashed on a spoon or the fingertip. If the baby doesn't care for banana, baked sweet potato or yam is a nutritious alternative.

Raw, peeled apple can be scraped with a spoon or grated. Cooked apples, pears, peaches, and apricots are excellent choices as well. Fruits such as plums, cherries, avocados, papayas, and peaches, can be pitted and blended with soaked, dried fruits, like apricots, dates, or sweet apple.

Acid fruits like citrus, berries, and tomatoes, should be avoided until the baby's first birthday. Canned fruits, with their high sugar content, should be avoided completely. Dried fruits, such as dates, figs, and raisins, are very sweet and sticky, and can contribute to tooth decay. They should not be given until the child can chew small pieces well - at about one year - and can floss and brush his or her teeth afterward (with a little help from a grownup).

2) **"Blender salads"** are then used to introduce the world of vegetables. Blend avocado with well-cooked greens and sesame butter (tahini), along with applesauce or maple syrup added for energy and sweetness. If the mixture is too thick, use vegetable juice to thin the mixture - sweet carrot works well. Legume protein, as tofu, or mashed, well-cooked beans or lentils can be added toward the end of the first year.

For "vitamin insurance," a dropper of iron-enriched multivitamins should be added to the blender daily, and then the creamy mixture offered to the baby, starting with **tiny** amounts at first - 1/4 teaspoon at a time.

Since vegan nutrition relies heavily upon green vegetables as calcium sources, blender salads and vegetable juices (celery, carrot, lettuce) can be started by age **seven months**, thus helping to avoid a possible aversion to dietary greens. Such foods supply protein, calcium, and other essential nutrients, while preparing the child to eat foods from the dinner table, which he or she will be doing by the end of the second year (and probably long before!)

Raw vegetables have more food value, and can be introduced at this time (7-8 months). However, they can be stringy and difficult to chew and digest. Don't be overly concerned if you find small bits of undigested vegetables in the baby's diaper. Grate the vegetables more finely, and decrease the amount per feeding. First exposure to "salad" vegetables in their whole form can be slices of tomato or avocado.

3) **Blended Cooked Vegetables** - At **seven** to **eight months**, cooked carrots, finely grated, mashed, or blended, can be introduced in a manner similar to apples. Carrots are especially rich in vitamins and calcium. Prepare cooked vegetables plainly, without salt, sugar, spices, or other additives. Parsnips, peas, sweet potatoes, asparagus, and squash, are also good introductory cooked vegetables. Blenderized sweet corn, raw or cooked, is a treat.

During these months, it is wise to avoid feeding **spinach** and **beets**, as they may contain excessive amounts of nitrates, potentially hazardous to infants under six months of age. Wait until at least ten months before introducing these vegetables.

Cabbage and its relatives, broccoli, brussels sprouts, and cauliflower, can cause problems with digestion if introduced too early - it is often best to wait until one year of age for this family of foods.

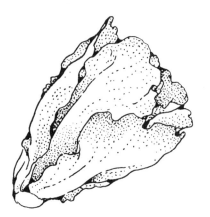  

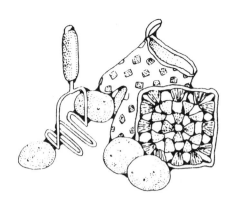

4) **Starchy foods**, like well-cooked potatoes, and cereals, are introduced towards the end of **nine months**.

Potatoes are wonderfully nutritious. They have a taste and consistency that babies love. Bake them whole to preserve vitamins, and mash with a small amount of water or breast milk. Mashing them with some cooked beets makes them "pink", much to the delight of infants.

Fortified whole grain cooked cereals, based upon oats, millet, rice, or barley, and sweetened with fruit juice, are preferable to precooked baby cereals, which are more expensive, and do not have the same nutritional value as homemade. If your family has a history of wheat or corn allergies, rice or oat cereals are usually safer. A small amount of mashed banana can be added to the cooked cereal to ease introduction to the baby.

At approximately one year of age, consider adding a "high protein cereal", with soybeans and wheat germ, available at the health food store; but be aware that soy and wheat products can induce food allergies when given too early. Make sure all cereals are quite liquid in consistency for easy digestibility.

5) **Legumes** (peas, beans, etc.) - usually are added toward the **end of the first year**, as will be described in the section entitled, "Using Beans for Human Beings." Sprouted garbanzo beans, and/or lentils, can be mashed, or put through a food mill, and added to blender salads or spread upon pieces of whole grain bread.

Be sure all beans are cooked until quite soft, and the bean skins (especially soybeans) are removed. A thin split pea soup is a good introduction to legume protein. Check the baby's stool to be sure the beans are not coming through undigested. If the stool smells sour, if the baby's bottom becomes reddened or irritated, or parts of beans are seen, wait a while before trying them again. Some children do not tolerate whole legumes until age 2 or 3, but that is okay. Other soy products (soy milk, tofu, etc.) and grains (breads, cereals, pastas, etc.) will meet all of the child's protein needs indefinitely.

At age 12 to 14 months, breads can be added, but small pieces of toast are easier for the baby to chew (gum!) and should be the form of bread given until the child is a "practiced chewer." And don't forget how much children, even young ones, love noodles. Pastas, enriched with artichoke flour and other whole grain flours, and served with gravies and sauces, provide extra energy and protein.

By age 14 to 18 months, children should be eating what their parents eat, (if necessary, after putting the food through the "baby food grinder") and will obtain all their nutritional requirements from the vegan foods listed in the "MEAL SUGGESTIONS" in the "Pregnancy" section.

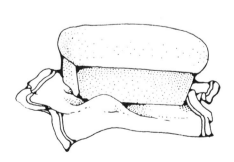
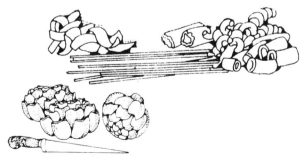

FOOD INTRODUCTION GUIDE

AGE (Approximate)	FOOD
Birth through 18 months	**BREAST MILK or** **SOY-BASED, VITAMIN-ENRICHED FORMULA**
2 to 3 months	**JUICES - Fruit, then vegetable**
6 to 7 months	**FRUITS - Bananas, cooked peaches, cooked applesauce** **Later: raw, grated apple, pear, apricot, plums, melons, soaked fruit** **Add liquid multivitamin/mineral supplement** (see text)
7 months	**"BLENDER SALADS" - Avocado, tofu, cooked greens, sprouts**
8 months	**COOKED VEGETABLES - Mashed, blended or grated carrots, parsnips, yams, squash**
10 months	**STARCHY FOODS- Potatoes, whole grain cereals (oats, millet, rice, barley, etc.)**
12 months	**"HIGH-PROTEIN" FOODS** **Wheat and soy cereals.** **Legumes - peas, beans, chick peas, lentils, soy products** **Nut butters - Almond, cashew, peanut**
14 through 18 months	**BREADS and PASTAS** **FAMILY DINNER FARE (pureed, if necessary)**

  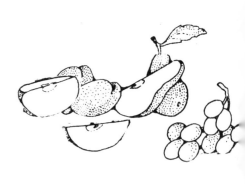

Here are some more thoughts about the "HOW" of

INTRODUCING SOLID FOODS

At five to six months, solid foods can be introduced, but still, there is no hurry to do this if the baby is content with nursing alone. Breast milk supplies the infant with complete nutrition through (and usually well past) age 6 months and the longer the mother waits to introduce solid foods, the less the chance of the baby developing food allergies. Early introduction of solid foods decreases the child's desire to nurse, and subsequently the mother's milk supply may lessen. If the baby is not content after breastfeedings, and is clearly "asking" for solids by crying and nipple chewing, it is probably time to start them.

When solid foods are introduced to a baby, they should be given one at a time; i.e., bananas only on a particular day, and then observe how well they are tolerated before adding more fruit or other food.

If two or more foods are introduced at the same time, and the baby has diarrhea, colic, or other digestive problems, you will not know which food caused the problem.

Give the baby's digestive system a few days (up to a week) to get used to each new food before introducing additional ones!

As for the timing of the first attempts at feeding solid food, if the baby is ravenously hungry, he may be in no mood to try anything new. For the first several weeks, try offering solids just after nursings. Two good times are mid-morning and mid-afternoon, when there are fewer worries about meals for the rest of the family.

Be patient and go slowly; this is practice time with food for the baby. Start with a 1/4 teaspoon of mashed banana at a time, holding the baby in your lap, tilting him back slightly as you touch the spoon to his lips and drop the food into his mouth. Show him by your smile that this is going to be something he'll like. Remember, these first attempts are merely to introduce him to solids, not to fill him up. He will let you know when he has had enough by turning his head away, clamping his mouth shut, or spitting the food back out. Take his word for it.

Remember, a little mess is all part of the game. If you plan for it, you won't be as irritated by baby's sloppiness and it will clean up more easily. Newspapers around the chair are a big help.

If baby isn't interested the first few times, just forget the whole project for another week, and then try again. Sometimes a baby doesn't get really interested in solids until eight or nine months. If he is healthy, there's no need to worry. Mother's milk will continue to be fully nourishing until he/she is ready to accept other food. Just continue to offer some solid food every now and then, and always be cheerful and pleasant when you do. Don't get frustrated or angry if the food is refused.

The further one gets away from food in its natural state, the poorer the food will be nutritionally. Dried or canned fruits will have less food value than fresh or frozen; refined cereals less than whole grain, and white rice less than brown (instant rice the least of all.)

Avoid all food for baby that contains sugar or artificial sweeteners. Sugar contains no vitamins, minerals, or protein, and contributes to obesity, which can affect a child for the rest of its life. It also confuses and seduces the appetite, since sweetened foods tend to satisfy hunger and displace healthful foods.

At the beginning, keep the items on the feeding tray very simple - one mound or piece of food in one unbreakable dish, and a small, unbreakable cup about a third filled with water or juice. Don't hesitate to "mix and match" foods that have already been introduced; often baby will view a new food with suspicion, but will accept it if it is mixed with one (s)he is already used to, and looks like the "one" food on the tray.

An inexpensive (approximately $10) "baby food grinder" can be invaluable for turning suitable table foods into a pureed texture for baby's digestive system. Remember, babies were eating mashed up food from their parents' table long before prepared baby food was put into little jars!

"Finger foods", for increasing control and coordination of hand, eye, (and mouth!), include mashed, cooked peas, chopped or mashed pieces of **well-steamed** carrot and broccoli, avocado slices, steamed potato pieces, mashed banana pieces, and peeled pear. Apricots, pineapple tidbits, and other fruits, are good for young mouths to nibble on, and can take the place of candy.

Throughout the child's early experiences with food, give him or her every opportunity to finger feed himself, but be ready to help with a spoon if it seems appropriate. When the baby wants to experiment with the spoon, offer encouragement and pick up another spoon for yourself.

Give the baby more of any food as he indicates he wants more. When he doesn't want more, stop. Don't coax, wheedle, cajole or force babies to eat. If they don't want to eat a certain food, try something else. Babies who are allowed free choice of only good, nutritious foods tend to balance their own diets.

The mother should always taste the food herself, but remember that she may have developed a taste for excessive salt or sugar. Babies' tongues should be gradually introduced to the subtleties of taste, rather than being assaulted by concentrated sugary and salty foods. With baby's food, bland is beautiful.

If a particular food seems to cause a reaction like skin rash, sore bottom, or mouth sores, eliminate that food for one week and then try again. If it has the same effect two or three times, discontinue it for at least six months.

Realize that humans, including babies, are social creatures. Your baby will eventually want to eat when the rest of the family does, rather than at off times. Try placing his chair next to yours at the table. He'll probably try to mimic what he sees the rest of the family doing; he will soon experiment with a dab of banana put on his high chair tray, especially if you maneuver so it seems to be coming right from your plate.

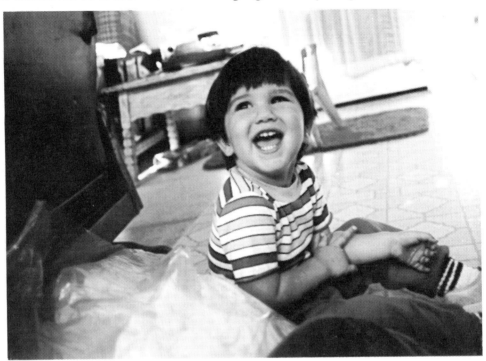

THOMAS EISMAN at 2 years, vegan from birth.

"CHEW CHEW" TRAIN

Infancy is the time when the good habit of thorough chewing can be most easily developed. Many problems with digestion and nutritional imbalance could be avoided if we masticate our food well.

Pass up teething biscuits, crackers, and pretzels, as they are "white starch" products with little food value. Toasted heels of whole wheat bread work well as a teething aid. Raw celery, carrot, or apple, are good foods upon which the older infant can practice chewing ("gumming"), but careful attention must be paid by the supervising adult to prevent choking mishaps.

Never leave infants unattended when food is in their grasp, as choking can occur suddenly. This warning includes peanut butter, apples, carrots, gluten, TVP products, and other similar foods. Teach your children to chew well, never to run with food in their mouths, and not to take bites too big.

All adults, especially new parents, should know how to clear an obstructed airway (trachea - air passage to the lungs) in both children and adults. Before an emergency occurs, obtain instruction from your family physician/pediatrician, and/or take a course in cardiopulmonary resuscitation (CPR) from the Red Cross.

FIBER

Avoiding Too Much of a Good Thing

The concern of nutritionists regarding nutrient availability for vegan children should be given due consideration. Excessive dietary fiber loads should be avoided in the diet of the growing child. Whole grains and legumes should still form the foundation of the daily meal plans, but to avoid excessive fiber loads:

l. Fruits and vegetables should be cooked with their skins on to preserve nutrients, and then **peeled** before serving.

2. Use liberal amounts of foods low in fiber, but high in calories or protein (having "**high nutrient density**"), such as **nut butters, tahini spread** (sesame seed butter), **chickpea hummus, pureed beans** mixed with **avocado** and/or nut butter, as well as "**blender salads**" (see "The Solid Food Parade").

During the day, children can be given the following "energy-packed" spreads, served on rice cakes, bread, or crackers.

Hummus, made with chickpeas and tahini, is a tasty food that toddlers love; it is rich in protein, calcium, and essential fats, and should be used to augment the infant's intake of these vital nutrients.

Avocado, rich in riboflavin, necessary vegetable fats, potassium, and copper, can be blended with a bit of water, fruit juice, or applesauce, to loosen its thick consistency.

Raw, unsalted nut butters (peanut, almond, cashew, etc.) are usually loved by children, and can even be spread on celery stalks and other raw vegetables to encourage the child to try new foods. Nut butters straight from the jar are often heavy and thus difficult for infants to digest. A practical serving idea is to mix a tablespoon or two of nut butter with a small quantity of water, or to blend with fruit juice or mashed fruit, thus converting the "butter" into a "cream."

3. Utilize some **refined grain products**, such as whole wheat pastry flour in breads and baked goods, refined rice or oat cereals, pastas, cous cous, etc.

4. Serve **fruit juices** for their calorie and vitamin content, as well as **fruit spreads** made from dried dates, apricots, raisins, etc., that are soaked overnight, blended, and served on bread or rice cake.

5. "**Full-fat**" **soy milk**, fortified with calcium and vitamins B-12 and D (see Appendix V - "Dairy Replacements"), should be used for drinking, and continued at least through age three to insure calories and fatty nutrients for developing the nervous system and other vital organs, as well as proper hormone balance.

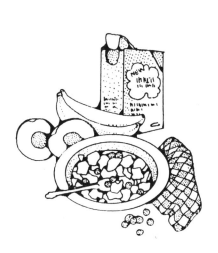

Nutritionists Dolores D. Truesdell and Phyllis Acosta, R.D., in their article, "Feeding the Vegan Infant and Child" (Journal of the American Dietetic Association, July, 1985, Vol. 85: No.7), while not endorsing vegan nutrition directly, provide two tables outlining practical diet plans for the vegan child.

The tables are presented here for their numerical values, which will be "brought to life" in the next section, "A Sample Day of Eating for an Active, Hungry Child."

Table 1. Diet plans for the vegan child

food group	approximate serving size*	daily servings per age group		
		6 mo-<1 yr	1-<4 yr	4-<6 yr
bread	1 sl, ½ pocket	1	3	4
cereals† (enriched)	1-5 Tbsp	½ (finely ground)	1	2
fats	1 tsp	0	3	4
fruits				
citrus	¼-½ c	0	2 (juice or chopped)	2
other‡	2-6 Tbsp	3 (pureed)	2 (chopped)	3
protein foods#	1-6 Tbsp	2 (cooked and sieved)	3 (chopped)	3
vegetables¶	¼-⅓ c			
green-leafy or deep yellow		¼ (cooked and pureed)	½ (chopped)	1
other		½ (cooked and pureed)	1 (chopped)	1
soy milk (fortified)‖	1 c	3	3	3
miscellaneous				
brewer's yeast**	1 Tbsp	0	1	1
molasses	1 Tbsp	0	1	1
wheat germ	1 Tbsp	0	optional	optional

*Applicable food composition data, specific portion sizes, suggestions on consistency, and information on individual foods used in this diet plan are available from the authors.
†Cereals include dry bulgur, corn flakes, wheat flakes, shredded wheat, enriched rice, millet, wild rice, macaroni, brown rice, wheat berries, dry oats, and granola.
†Cereals fortified with vitamin B-12 may be acceptable to the strict vegetarian.
‡Other fruits include avocado, apple, peach, banana, pear, berries, apricots, and grapes. Dried fruit spreads include those made with dried peaches, apricots, raisins, and figs.
#Protein foods include nuts, nut butters, peanut butter, legumes, miso, seeds, seed butters, and tofu. Legumes include soybeans, peanuts, black beans, black-eyed peas, pintos, and split peas. Nuts include almonds, cashews, pignolia, walnuts, pecans, and pistachios. Seeds include pumpkin, sesame, and sunflower. Nuts and seeds should be ground for the toddler. Nut milks may be made for older children but should not replace soy milk.
¶Deep-yellow and dark-green leafy vegetables include carrots, green peppers, broccoli, spinach, endive, escarole, and kale. Other vegetables include bean sprouts, potatoes, tomatoes, lettuce, cabbage, corn, celery, snap beans, onions, cucumbers, beets, and cauliflower. Bean sprouts include mung, soy, and alfalfa. Potatoes include white potato and sweet potato, baked and boiled.
‖Fortified soy milks include Isomil, Nursoy, ProSobee, and Soyalac. Data were obtained from Wyeth Laboratories and Ross Laboratories and/or labels.
**Nutritional yeast is not an appropriate food for the infant. The purine content may be greater than 150 mg/100 gm. Yeast does not naturally contain vitamin B-12. Golden Harvest's Potent Yeast (distributed by Natural Sales Co., Pittsburgh) is fortified with vitamin B-12. Other specially grown yeast or fortified products are available; the amounts of vitamin B-12 vary.

Table 2. Proximate nutritive value of basic diet plans for vegan children

age (yr)	energy*		protein		riboflavin		vitamin B-12†		vitamin D‡		calcium		iron		zinc#	
	kcal	% RDA	gm	% RDA	mg	% RDA	μg	% RDA	μg	% RDA	mg	% RDA	mg	% RDA	mg	% RDA
0.5-<1	891	94	28	155	0.75	125	1.8	120	7.4	74	579	107	14.1	94	5.9	118
1-<4	1,330	102	43	160	1.32	165	1.8	90	7.4	74	905	113	19.3	129	8.6	86
4-<6	1,592	94	48	160	1.46	146	1.8	72	7.4	74	960	120	21.4	214	9.6	96

*The energy content of the diet could be substantially increased with more liberal use of dried fruits, cereals, and nut butters.
†The B-12 content of the diet could be increased with B-12 supplements, fortified brewer's yeast, or fortified cereal. If the 4- to 6-year-old consumed only fortified soy milk, he or she would obtain only 72% of the RDA for vitamin B-12.
‡Vitamin D status is improved by exposure to sunlight and by the use of fortified margarines.
#The zinc content of the diet could be increased by including wheat germ, fortified cereals, and brewer's yeast.

LIBERTY PHOENIX, actress, vegan, at age 9.

A SAMPLE DAY OF EATING
FOR AN ACTIVE, HUNGRY CHILD

To illustrate the high nutritional value of vegan cuisine for children, let's see how the sample meals described below will supply the child's requirements for protein, calcium, and iron. To allow for the smaller nutritional needs of children, the following figures are based upon one-half portion servings, and were derived by halving the nutrient values of the meals in Appendix II.

Recipes for six additional days of vegan meals are given in Appendix III.

Breakfast - 1 ounce Whole Grain Cereal with Almonds and Raisins
topped with (3 ounces) Soy or Sunflower Milk
1 slice Whole Grain Toast with 1 tablespoon Peanut Butter.

PROTEIN: 7.5 g. CALCIUM 100 mg. IRON 1.75 mg.

Lunch - Medium Garden Green Salad with 1 tablespoon Tahini Dressing,
1 cup Soup (Vegetable/Bean, Rice, Lentil, etc.) and
1 Sandwich (3 ounces) Hummus spread with Lettuce, Sprouts, Tomato
and Tahini Sauce, 2 slices Whole Grain Bread.

PROTEIN 20 g. CALCIUM 300 mg. IRON 7 mg.

Dinner - 1 medium Garden Green or Carrot Salad,
1 cup Whole Grain or "Artichoke" Spaghetti,
3 tablespoons Tomato/Mushroom/TVP Sauce;
1 cup chopped, steamed Broccoli or Collards
2 tablespoons Tahini or Nutritional Yeast Gravy.

PROTEIN 13 g. CALCIUM 300 mg. IRON 5 mg.

Desserts and Treats - 1/2 cup Almond and Raisin Mix, or
a 4-ounce glass of calcium and Vitamin D-enriched Soymilk (Edensoy, Ah Soy, etc.)
2 Oatmeal/Raisin Cookies, **or**
4-ounce Fruit Smoothie enriched with 2 ounces Tofu, **or**
Peanut Butter and Fruit Spread Sandwich on Whole Grain Bread, etc.

Each will supply an additional:

PROTEIN 5 g. CALCIUM 100 mg. IRON 2 mg.

Such a day of eating will supply a growing child under age 10, with over 45 grams of gently-absorbed, high quality plant protein, for growth, over 800 mg. of calcium for strong bones, and over 15 milligrams of iron to make healthy blood, ALL WITHOUT EATING MEAT OR DAIRY PRODUCTS!

RAINBOW PHOENIX, television and film actress, vegan, age 14.

CHILDHOOD AND ADOLESCENCE

As kids get older, they will love breakfasts of fruit bowls, whole grain cereals with sunflower milk, chopped almonds and raisins, or scrambled tofu with toast and peanut butter. Lunches with grainburgers served on whole wheat buns with "all the trimmings" are usually big hits with young people. Dinners of vegetable soups with whole grain bread, Chinese or Italian-style entrees (stir-fried vegetables over rice, tofu lasagna, spaghetti with tomato sauce, etc.), or burgers, served in small portions, will soon become "childhood favorites". Children introduced to healthful vegan dishes early in life will grow up viewing non-animal foods as "normal" and delicious, preferable to fatty meats, dairy products, and "junk foods."

By age 12, the young person will usually begin to eat adult portions, (often larger!) with adult taste preferences. (At this time, the person buying the food will usually give thanks for the inexpensive ingredients of the vegan diet. Grains, beans and vegetables will always cost less than meat and dairy products!)

For treats, sweets, and desserts, think of fruits: grapes, peaches, apples, pears, bananas, strawberries, blueberries, etc. Try mixing them together in a "fruit bowl", topped with sunflower seeds and fruit juice, with a sprinkle of cinnamon. Melon slices or grapefruit sections are good candy substitutes, as are dried apricots, prunes, pineapple, raisins, apples, pears, etc. Fruit smoothies, including the Banana-Tahini "Malted", take the place of milk-shakes. Peanut, almond, sunflower seed, and raisin mix is a perennial snack favorite. In addition, tofu yogurt, frozen banana "nice cream", vegan baked goods (like apple pie, whole grain muffins, cookies, banana bread, etc.) can be enjoyed for nutritious treats.

Such a daily eating style will easily meet or exceed requirements for protein, calcium, iron and other vital nutrients. Remember, additional protein, calcium, and iron can always be added to the child's diet with "Nutrition Boosters" like oatmeal cookies, granola with soymilk, peanut butter and fruit spread sandwich on whole grain bread, a hummus (chick pea spread) sandwich on pita bread, an extra handful of chopped almonds and raisins, or a piece of last night's tofu lasagna. Texturized vegetable protein (TVP), available at all health food stores, are dry granules of soy protein that, when mixed with water, become small, chewy nuggets that can be added to spaghetti sauce, chili, casseroles, and soups, and greatly increase the protein value of the dish.

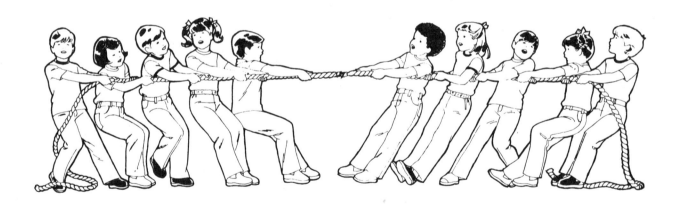

Remember, children tend to eat smaller amounts, but more frequently during the day. There should be an "open door policy" for easy access to the refrigerator. It should be stocked with healthy foods within reach for the child. Pay attention to the weather; heat will influence the child's needs and desires, as will a colder climate or a rainy day. Once children realize that vegan cuisine is the "proper" food to eat, they will find favorite foods among the many selections, and ask for, and appreciate healthful main dishes and snacks.

DO KIDS NEED VITAMIN SUPPLEMENTS?

I believe that it is possible to raise a healthy child on wholesome, natural foods without him or her ever taking a vitamin tablet. Children have been growing up throughout history long before vitamin supplements were invented.

A child raised in the country, with a nearby garden supplying organically grown produce, is indeed fortunate. However, few children have access to such a wonderful resource. They must rely upon commercially available produce and processed foods, whose vitamin content may be less than the child needs for optimum health.

Thus, although fresh fruits and vegetables are the best sources of vitamins and minerals, and deficiencies of vitamins are unlikely with balanced vegan nutrition, "vitamin insurance" through supplementation is recommended for growing children and adolescents.

SOLOMON COOPER, vegan from birth, at 18 months.

VITAMIN B-12

Vitamin B-12 is made (only) by **bacteria** that live in the soil, and within our mouths and intestines. The liver stores vitamin B-12, and thus acts as a B-12 "buffer."

Vitamin B-12 is necessary for development of red blood cells and proper nerve function, as well as being essential for normal growth of height and weight. Parents raising their children as vegans must assure that adequate amount of Vitamin B-12 are available in the food. The three most common ways to assure B-12 adequacy are as follows:

(a) Utilize foods that have been **fortified** with B-12. These include fortified cereals, breads, "soymeat" products and various soymilks. Nutritional yeast* and tempeh contain **variable** amounts of vitamin B-12 and should not be relied upon as sole sources of this vitamin. Read the product labels to see if "Vitamin B-12" or "cyanocobalamin" has been added, and that the amount averages at least 2 - 3 micrograms daily.

(b) The family's cook can crush two 25-microgram tablets of Vitamin B-12 and add some of the crushed powder to salad dressings, soups, juices, mashed fruits, or soy milk, several times per week.

(c) The child may be given a B-12 containing vitamin supplement as suggested in "Supplemental Advice".

"Getting enough Vitamin B-12"
should never be a rationale for feeding meat or dairy products to a child.

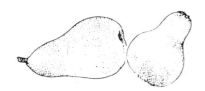

RIBOFLAVIN

(Vitamin B-2)

This important vitamin, vital for energy production, is found in **wheat germ, soy beans, leafy green vegetables, nutritional yeast, avocados** (an especially rich source), **almonds, and fortified soy formula** for infants. The vegan diet that contains these foods should meet all needs for riboflavin, but again, a dropperful of a vitamin supplement would erase all doubts.

VITAMIN D

As presented in the "Pregnancy" section, Vitamin D is required for calcium absorption from our intestines, and is actually a hormone made by our own body when **sunlight** falls upon the skin. Vitamin D needs can be met through exposing a child's skin to sunshine for 15 minutes each day; we really don't need to ingest it in our diet at all. This vitamin, made during summer sun months and stored by the liver, can last through the winter. Rickets (soft, calcium-poor bones from Vitamin D deficiency), should never occur in vegan children given the opportunity to walk or play out in the sunshine every day for at least fifteen minutes. Thus, even on a cold winter's day, time spent to enjoy thirty minutes of sunshine through an open window (with a southern exposure) is important to the child for nutritional, as well as emotional and psychological reasons. When weather permits, babies can be brought outside for naps, feeding, and exploring times. Mothers can share sun time with their children while performing usual "inside" tasks, such as reading, eating, or preparing vegetables for dinner.

Vegan children living in northern climates who may have difficulty in obtaining their fifteen minutes of daily sun time, should receive supplemental vitamin D (ergosterol) at least during the winter, in the form of vitamin supplements or enriched soy milk. As excessive amounts of vitamin D can be toxic, the total daily amount should be restricted to 400 I.U. (See "Pregnancy" section re: Vitamin D supplements.)

---

*Nutritional yeast, due to its concentration of purines (nucleic acids), which can possibly tax the kidneys of infants, should not be added to the diet until age 12 months. From 6 months, vegan infants should be given liquid multivitamins containing B-12.

CALCIUM

A vegan child should be asssured of adequate intake of calcium which, fortunately, abounds in most plants. After all, cows get their calcium from eating green plants, not from drinking cow's milk.

Most vegan children should not require a calcium supplement. Parents should help their child learn to iden--tify and enjoy the "calcium champs" in vegan nutrition, which include the following:

1) **Greens** - broccoli, collards, kale, mustard greens, etc.

2) **Legumes** - tofu, chickpeas, beans.

3) **Seeds** - sunflower, sesame/tahini, pumpkin.

4) **Nuts** - almonds, filberts, cashews, nut butters.

Other sources include oranges, raisins, figs, dates, apricots, molasses, and some drinking water ("hard water" contains calcium).

For snacking, offer high-calcium chickpea/tahini hummus, which children love spread on bread. The almond/raisin/sunflower seed mix left out for kids to snack upon will also boost their intake of calcium, protein and iron.

From birth through one year, the calcium contained in breastmilk or fortified soy milk formula, will supply adequate calcium, up to 500 mgs. per day.

However, at age one year, if there is any question of calcium adequacy in the diet, liquid calcium supplements can be added to juices, soups, and other foods, to bring total calcium intake up to recommended amounts. The calcium should probably be in the "ascorbate" form (combined with vitamin C - see your pharmacist or health food store attendant), and also combined with a balancing amount of magnesium - approximately 250 milligrams of magnesium to each 500 milligrams of calcium.

Read the label on the calcium supplement to determine the amount of calcium in each teaspoon, and add the appropriate amounts according to the following guidelines:

Age (years)	Average Calcium from Food (mgs.)	Suggested Amount of Supplemental Calcium (mgs.)	Total (mgs.)
1 to 3	400	400	800
4 to 6	500	300	800
7 to 10	500	300	800
11 to 21	1000	250	1200

Remember, the calcium-rich foods in vegan cuisine, combined with the low protein (and thus calcium-sparing) nature of the diet, produces strong bones for vegan children, who have less osteoporosis as adults.

   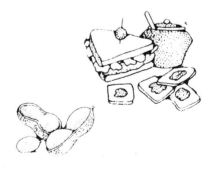

IRON

Iron supplies must be ample to keep pace with the child's production of new blood. The **iron-containing greens, legumes, whole and enriched grains, molasses, and dried fruits**, like apricots, raisins, and dates, already presented, should meet most needs for iron. Blending well-cooked greens with some raisins and molasses, makes an "iron cocktail" that toddlers and older children enjoy spread on rice cakes or mixed with grains. A 50 or 100 mg. tablet of Vitamin C added to the blender would enhance iron absorption.

At five to six months, the baby's iron stores should be tested with a blood count (by finger-stick method). If iron deficiency (anemia) is found, iron supplement drops are recommended. After eight months, iron-enriched, processed rice cereals (pablum) can be introduced.

Cow's milk has been shown to irritate the intestines of many children and actually induce low-grade bleeding from the bowel wall. This steady loss of blood can contribute to childhood anemia, and milk drinking should always be suspected and eliminated as a cause of anemia.[126]

There is no need to eat red meats, liver or other flesh foods to "get enough iron."

ZINC

Zinc, necessary for adequate growth, healthy skin, and a strong immune system, is found in **fortified cereals, whole grains, green leafy vegetables, mushrooms, nuts, seeds (especially sesame/tahini), legumes, tofu, miso, wheat germ,** and **nutritional yeast**.

Although dietary sources of zinc are probably adequate, there should be no doubt of sufficient supplies of this essential element to the growing child. Therefore, read the label of the multivitamin/mineral supplement given to the child, to be sure it contains the following amounts of zinc:

6 months/1 year: 5 mg./day
1 year to 10 years: 10 mg./day
11 years to adult: 15 mg./day

If these amounts of zinc are not present, a separate zinc supplement should be added. Powdered zinc tablets or a liquid preparation can be added to gravies, salad dressings, fruit smoothies, etc.

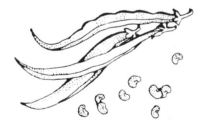

FATS

ESSENTIAL FATTY ACIDS

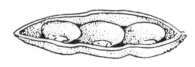

These oily substances are necessary for health of skin, nerve, blood, in production of adrenal and other hormones, and for the growth of the child. All fatty nutrients essential for human health are found in the oils of plants, especially **whole grains, legumes, nuts, seeds, and cooking oils**, like olive, peanut, and safflower.

Some children, (especially if they are eating animal fats in processed foods and fatty meats, which block absorption of the "good" plant oils), can suffer deficiencies of these vital oils that create healthy skin and hormones. A child with signs of oil deficiency, i.e., dry skin, lusterless hair, dandruff, splitting nails, or excessive irritability, would probably benefit from 1/2 teaspoon of (food-grade!) linseed oil, daily, on bread or mixed with food. This should be continued until better oil balance is created in the diet by increasing the amounts of sunflower seeds, olive oil, avocados, nut butters, etc. (along with eliminating animal fats which interfere with normal fatty acid function).

SOREN WAGNER, California vegan, at 2 months.

Vegan beachcomber JIMMY PEDEN at 3 years.

61

"SUPPLEMENTAL" ADVICE

To provide "insurance" of adequate vitamin intake for toddlers, one dropperful of commercial vitamins (Solgar "Nutrifort Liquid", Poly-Vi-Sol with Iron, Vi-Daylin Plus Iron Drops, or other similar supplement) can and should be added to the "blender salad" or other "toddler" food each day until the child's intake of fresh vegetables is obviously adequate. Such supplementation will provide 400 I.U. of Vitamin D, 1.5 micrograms of B-12, 10 mgs. iron, and .6 mgs. of riboflavin - the nutrients of greatest concern for vegan children.

During childhood and adolescence, a standard children's (vegetarian) multivitamin and mineral preparation is advised 3 to 6 times weekly, especially to insure vitamin B-12 adequacy.

Insuring adequate iron supplies has already been presented and, if indicated by finger-stick blood count, liquid iron supplements should be employed.

Calcium supplements should be given, if necessary, as discussed in that section.

The supplements listed above will provide "vitamin insurance" for the growing child. Again, (and for the last time) there is no justification for including meat or dairy products in the child's diet to obtain "essential vitamins", or "other nutrients." The reports from parents raising their children as vegans provide us all with reassurance and encouragement, as presented in the **"Proof of the Pudding...Good News from Vegan Parents"** section which follows.

SWEET NOTES

A child whose parents are guiding him or her away from the standard, fast food "Great American Dietary Catastrophe", should not be made to feel that he or she is being deprived. Children and sweets seem to be inseparable, and the vegan diet has many delights that will satisfy anyone's sweet tooth. However, the proper attitude toward sweets needs to be developed early. If your kids beg for candy and gum in the store, the best thing to do is not to give in. When the candy cravings hit home, start making your own, using the recipes for "carob balls", fudge, and other delights found in the numerous available vegan cookbooks.

Use carob powder freely; it will become preferred to chocolate as kids get older. "Chocolate" fudge can be made in the blender or food processor, using carob powder, peanut butter, water, and a sweetener like sorghum or maple syrup. This fudge can be used as cake icing, dessert topping, or frozen for a solid sweet treat. A nutritious "chocolate" drink can be made by adding carob powder to sunflower milk in the blender for "carob sunny milk."

For an ice cream substitute, try freezing peeled, ripe bananas, cut into cylinders and serve them with tahini topping or non-dairy carob fudge. Half a banana on a popsicle stick, or a favorite fruit juice poured into an ice tray, can be frozen as fun treats - and are simple to make. Freezing a fruit smoothie creates a delicious sherbet.

Non-dairy "yogurt" can be quickly made in the blender with tofu, frozen fruit and fruit juice, and its taste is free of the "sour quality" of dairy yogurt. Tofu yogurt can also be frozen and eaten at a later date.

Recently, several brands of non-dairy frozen desserts (Rice Dream, some flavors of Tofutti, etc.) have appeared in the freezer cases of most health food stores and many supermarkets. Though "novelty" foods, and best enjoyed in moderation, they are far preferable to standard fat and additive-laden ice cream and dairy desserts.

Help children to moderate their sweet intake, and be sure to help the child learn to clean (floss and brush) his or her teeth after eating sweets.

For general sweetening purposes, **avoid using honey**. It is an insect food, not intended for humans, and has been responsible for cases of fatal **botulism** in infants[125].

Sweeteners like maple syrup, barley malt, rice syrup (yinny), date sugar, and sorghum are preferable, while shredded coconut, chopped nuts and seeds, fruit juices, concentrated fruit syrup, and fruits like raisins, dates, and pineapple, can serve as sweeteners in many recipes.

WHAT ABOUT BIRTHDAY PARTIES?

Problems can arise when the vegan child attends a birthday party at a non-vegan household. Sending vegan baked goods and treats with your child helps to alleviate this problem. If you do not have the opportunity to explain the vegan rationale to the host's parents, to avoid awkward situations, some parents notify the hosts that their children are on special diets, and thus will be bringing their own treats. When the vegan child has a birthday, numerous sweets, including an eggless, dairyless, birthday cake, can be prepared for everyone to enjoy.

Vegan cuisine, as presented in many excellent vegan cookbooks, offers many baked treats like cookies, cakes, apple pie and banana bread, all made without eggs, sugar, or dairy products.

MORE NOURISHING IDEAS

1. Children are not born with a taste for "junk foods." Such tastes are **acquired**, many times from the foods they are given at parties, at friends' houses, and at school. Of course, sweet desserts brought home from the store by parents are the biggest temptation for children. Avoid starting your child down the health-destroying road of fast foods (fat-foods), white sugar and flour products, and other seductive sweets. If the harmful foods are not purchased and brought into your house, the children will be less likely to eat them.

If your young person aleady has a taste for burgers, milk shakes, etc., learn more about the many delicious alternatives (grain burgers with all the trimmings, tofu pizzas, spaghetti, and lasagnas, banana "malteds", carob treats, etc.) offered by vegan cuisine, and begin to offer these tasty dishes along with, and then instead of, the fast food fare. You will be amazed at how quickly your child learns to ask for these healthy meals and treats.

2. **Never let your dinner table become a battlefield!** Avoid getting locked into a test of wills with your child as to whether, what, and when he or she will eat. Invite your child to the table as a member of the family, but if he or she does not want to eat, **do not argue.** Rather, lovingly show him/her (as you put the food away in the refrigerator), that the meal is waiting, and when the child gets hungry enough to eat, you will be glad to put it back on the table. Don't worry, your child will not starve to death; hunger is a powerful motivator, and a young person will eventually ask for dinner. The child will soon learn that dinnertime is for eating.

3. To avoid the excessive loads of sugars and fats that are found in most school cafeteria foods, pack your child a good lunch to take with him/her, like hearty sandwiches, a thermos of soup, a plastic container of salad, and healthy treats for dessert. Your child will be less tempted by junk foods, will stay healthier, and will set an example of good nutrition for the other children.

Be aware that there may be pressure upon your child from teachers and fellow students to eat foods from the "Four Food Groups", including meat and dairy products. From your confidence that vegan nutrition is fully balanced and nourishing, pressure to consume animal foods can be dissipated by keeping the vegan issue low-key (but firm in your resolve), as well as packing along a thermos of soy milk and a grainburger that **looks** like cafeteria food, but certainly is not.

The climate is becoming more favorable towards healthful foods being provided by school meal programs. If you have a child in the public school system, you can be instrumental in making the cafeteria increase its offerings of health-producing foods.

There have already been success stories in numerous cities of salad bars in elementary school cafeterias, and the removal of candy machines from high school lunchrooms. It is possible to replace cola drinks with fruit juices, and candy bars with dried and fresh fruit desserts. The school systems, though slow to change, are becoming aware that nutrition for their students is in need of improvement. Work with them to raise the quality of school lunches. Of course, the more vegan entrees, side dishes, and desserts placed on the menu, the better.

4. Remember, "the child is the father (or mother) of the adult". What we feed our children sets the pattern for health or disease throughout the rest of their lives. Children learn by example; if the parents eat healthy, non-animal foods, it is easier to instill eating habits that the young ones will follow.

5. Children seem to be naturally appalled when they first learn that the chicken or lamb they are eating was actually a proud chicken or cuddly lamb that they have loved. This reaction is a pure and natural one and should be a lesson for both the child and the adult preparing their food. The deeper aspects of a diet free of animal flesh and milk are important topics that provide opportunites for loving discussion and exploration by family members.

6. Children require more than just pure nutrition to become healthy, happy adults. Growing up in a loving environment, where the parents speak lovingly to each other and settle differences constructively, is key to shaping a gentle character. Children should be introduced to wholesome music early and learn to play non-violent games. Toys and television programs should be selected by both the parents and the child to be as free from violence, and exploitative sex-role stereotyping as possible.

Parents should accompany their children on walks through the park, forest preserve, or other green settings, to foster love for the natural world. Early, frequent contact with gentle animals reaffirms the child's natural feelings of love and protectiveness. Helping a child grow up as an open, strong, exploring, and sensitive person is one of the greatest gifts any parent can give.

OCEAN ROBBINS, Vegan Son of Author John Robbins & wife Deo has never tasted any meat.

A champion marathon racer, he set his school record for push-ups and pullups, and at age 10, was a nationally -ranked distance runner for 10 km.

Ocean is taller than many of his friends of the same age, enjoyed excellent health and has never seen a physician for a serious illness.

"PROOF OF THE PUDDING"

GOOD NEWS FROM VEGAN PARENTS

It is important for parents raising vegan children to know that they are not taking risks with the nutritional health of their children. It is always reassuring to learn of the success other vegan parents have had in creating healthy, happy vegan children. Here are some families you should know about:

Marcia Pearson, well-known fashion model and activist on behalf of rights for people and animals, and her gymnast/husband Kent McCormack, are the parents of Tahira, born in the Spring of 1984. Marcia, who has enjoyed a vegan diet for years, experienced a successful pregnancy, labor and delivery without problem or undue stress. Both Marcia and Tahira thrived after the birth, and Marcia takes pleasure in relating how Tahira destroys the stereotypes of "underweight" and "undersized" vegan kids. She writes:

"...I think the vegan baby thing (about them being smaller) is a fallacy. Tahira's birth weight and size was perfectly normal - 7 pounds, 5 ounces, and 21.5 inches long. From about 5 months on, she was considerably larger than other babies her age, but never "fat." From age 1 to age 2, she grew at a very fast pace. At age 2, she weighed 38 pounds and was 3 feet tall. At 2 1/2, her language skills were like that of a 4-year old, and her memory was better than her parents'! She is very active during the day, and sleeps 8 to 10 hours a night, but sometimes even less.

So far, Tahira is bigger than all her peers...including many three year olds, and one doctor said she was the most muscular kid he'd ever seen and definitely the largest for two years old.

He observed her behavior and told us we should start her on music or dance lessons right away (she was singing songs for everyone). He said her sense of rhythm, coordination and voice was like that of a four or five year old. Naturally, we told him she is vegan and we got into long discussions of, 'where does she get her protein or calcium?'

After about twenty minutes of dialogue he said, 'Well, you must be doing something right!', and said he would definitely look into this "vegan business." Other parents are always guessing her to be one to two years older than she is, also... she really is a shining example of veganism - especially her mental and physical development.

So, while I'll happily agree that vegan babies are brighter, I will totally disagree that they are smaller. The physical stature of the parents is the greater determinant of size rather than nutrition. Health has nothing to do with big, small, or medium build. So give babies lots of good grub and love, and they'll be what size they should be."

THOMAS EISMAN,

Florida lifelong vegan, age 2.

George Eisman, R.D., is a registered dietician and formerly headed the Vegetarian Studies curriculum at Miami-Dade Community College, Miami, Florida. George and Shelly are raising their son, Thomas, on pure vegan nutrition, and he is thriving. Breast-fed from birth, solid foods were introduced at six months as cooked bananas and peaches, followed by well-cooked vegetables (sweet potato, carrots, soft greens), then cereals, breads and pastas, and finally, legumes (tofu, etc.) At eleven months, Thomas was happy, bright, active, taking his first steps, and sharing most of George's and Shelly's food from the dinner table.

Thomas is given no vitamin supplements and so far has been free of colds, ear infections, runny noses, and similar childhood problems. He has never been given dairy products or refined sugars, and as any observer will note by watching him at mealtime, Thomas thinks vegan food is wonderful.

VICTORIA MORAN

with her daughter, RACHAEL.

WILLOW JAY BASTONE

at 9 months, vegan since birth.

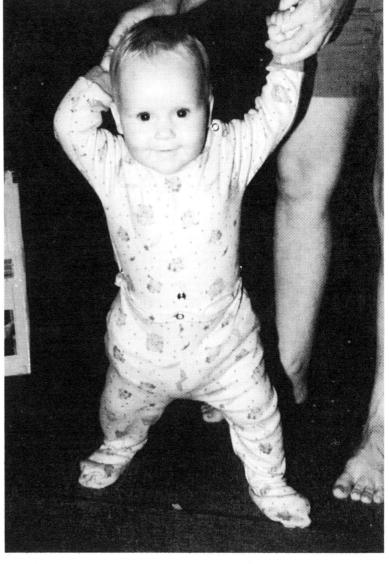

67

Authoress (of Compassion, the Ultimate Ethic) and journalist, **Victoria Moran**, is learning a great deal from raising her daughter, Rachael, as a vegan. Victoria shares the following:

"As I write this, my daughter Rachael is nearly five years old. In the time she has been with me, I have learned from both my successes and failures in attempting to raise a vegan child. The main things I've done right--and would do again with another child--include:

(1) Extended breastfeeding with "baby-led weaning" and active involvement with La Leche League;

(2) Development of friendships with other vegan/vegetarian families;

(3) Much open communication with the child about my beliefs and practices from early toddlerhood;

(4) Clear explanation of my stand to relatives who are well-meaning but ignorant on this subject; and

(5) Using children's books--the few that are available--to support my stand on animal rights and a healthful, natural diet. I have found books such as, I Love Animals & Broccoli, from the Baltimore Vegetarian Society, The Fruit & Vegetable Lover's Coloring Book, by Victoria Bidwell, and many of the library books listed in Barbara Friedman's bibliography, Animals, Kids and Books (available from Amberwood, Route 1, Box 206, Milner, GA 30257), to be of inestimable assistance.

I also slip in little messages from time to time like, 'Mr. Rogers is vegetarian like us, you know!' and 'Michael Jackson is a strict vegan!'

Other things I've learned is to keep our meals simple and filled with love and joy, and that example is much more powerful than instruction."

Pat Bastone is president of the Vancouver Island Vegetarian Association (VIVA). At Christmas of 1985, Pat and her husband, George, welcomed Willow Jay into the world. She gives the following account of the birth:

"When I was fully dilated, my doctor said, 'Go ahead', and I just went at it! I had a lot of energy, and everyone thought I did great - it was fun and exciting from that point on. At 9:25 P.M., Willow Jay was placed on my tummy, and we were all surprised at how large she was - 8 pounds, 2 ounces! I was really pleased because I didn't look that big, and I'm sure that a lot of my non-vegetarian family and friends thought I was going to produce a tiny, anemic-looking babe!

Willow Jay has inherited her daddy's appetite! I nursed her 1/2 hour after she was born. She was wide awake, very alert, and George was/is absolutely thrilled. My mom and dad came down to the hospital to hold her one hour after birth - it was really nice.

When we brought Willow home, she weighed 7 pounds, 13 ounces, and at 24 days old, weighed in at 10 pounds, 6 ounces! (Author's medical note - many/most newborn infants lose weight, mostly water, in the first few days of life, but regain this weight quickly as they nurse). She's outgrowing everything so fast! We are so pleased at how well both she and I are doing."

At press time, Pat sent the following update:

"Willow weighed 8 lbs., 2 oz., and measured 21" at birth, and has exceeded average growth rates in both weight and height. She gained 17 oz. in her first 9 days at home, weighed 22 lbs. at 9 months, and now at 14 1/2 months, is close to 30 lbs. She was completely breastfed by me, nursing on demand, till 5 1/2 months, when she started showing interest in our food. We then started her on drinking apple juice from a cup. She has never had a pacifier or bottle. She still nurses and we plan to let her lead the weaning. She has never had supplements.

She now enjoys: millet, cream of wheat, rice, barley, rice crackers, soy milk, whole wheat toast and tahini, peanut butter, homemade lentil/vegetable soup, buckwheat noodles, kale, spinach, carrots, avocado, fruits, and especially loves apples, grapes, tempeh, malted soy milk, tofu pudding, macaroni & "cheez" (made with nutritional yeast), and her grandma's carob cake.

The only health problems have been a couple of minor colds and an ear infection at 8 months which quickly cleared up with antibiotics.

Willow's front teeth came in at 6 - 8 months, and she is now getting a good crop of molars. Teething has not affected her happy disposition.

"Ma Ma" was Willow's first word at 6 months, and she now has a vocabulary of 7 words with her own "words" or body gestures for many more - e.g., sniffing for "flowers." She walked at a year old, having been a "bum shuffler" before that, not a crawler (apparently all the kids in my family got around that way).

She is plump, tall for her age, very sociable, loves animals especially "bow-wa's", and is crazy about books. She has a great sense of humour and an infectious giggle.

Our family doctor, who supervised my pregnancy and attended Willow's birth, is a lifelong vegetarian (very close to vegan), and raising his two kids as vegetarians of course. I really appreciate his support in giving Willow (and George and I) a diet that I know is just the best for her health and is in harmony with her own joyous and life-ful spirit."

THE PHOENIX FAMILY

The vegan PHOENIX family.

The Phoenix Family - John and Arlyn Phoenix have raised their five children as vegans largely for reasons of ethics and compassion. As Arlyn says, "We are vegetarians because we don't believe in oppressing animals. We believe in gentleness, kindness, honesty and truth. That's why our children, while having careers in show business, never did commercials for soda and junk food. You can't compromise your soul."

The Phoenix children, River, Rainbow, Leaf, Liberty and Summer, all healthy and active, ranging (at the time of this printing) from seventeen to ten years of age, respectively, have created careers in Hollywood films and entertainment. Their success stories have been featured in many magazines ("Life", "People", "Vegetarian Times", "Seventeen", "USA Today"), and on numerous television programs. The Phoenix family's desire for non-violence in their diets and lifestyles, and the examples they set, have earned them special recognition on the movie sets where the children work.

The health advantages of a vegan diet show clearly in the Phoenix children, as they take no medications, have no allergies or serious illnesses, have never been hospitalized, take no vitamin supplements, and have not needed a physician's services.

John and Arlyn offer these reflections to parents: "Raising your child vegan is a wonderful blessing for all the family. Introducing a lifestyle of harmlessness and gentleness is such a beautiful beginning, and children accept this as natural, as indeed it is. The respect that they feel in their hearts for all living creatures is a very important step to higher consciousness. The blessing of good health is the "topping on the cake". We have found this moral commitment encourages children to stay vegan as they grow up, as it is an affair of the heart which children can relate to, rather than for reasons of good health, which isn't a priority with the youth.

Ideas for "first foods" after breastfeeding: Fresh juice from a Champion juicer, strained very well and diluted with water. Next, mashed bananas and blended fruit.

On the best food to have on hand for toddlers: Fruits, frozen fruits for sherbet, nuts, and dried fruits.

For teens: Tofu, frozen fruits for desserts, carob flavored treats, nuts, and dried fruits.

On feeding children on the road: "The Phoenix kids have been 'on the road' all their lives - with avocado, tahini, peanut butter, tofu, rice cakes, fresh fruits, and veggies. It's a snap to eat vegan food wherever you are."

John and Arlyn report that their children encountered some resistance among their peers, but, "the children were always proud to stand up for the rights of animals, and have thus influenced many of their friends to eat an animal-free diet."

The Phoenix children have all been featured in television series and major motion pictures. River Phoenix appeared in "Stand By Me", "Mosquito Coast" with Harrison Ford, "Little Nikita", with Sidney Poitier, and "Running On Empty"; Leaf Phoenix in "Space Camp", and in "Russkies", along with sister, Summer; Rainbow Phoenix in "Maid to Order", with vegetarian actress, Ally Sheedy; and seem destined to be vegan superstars.

AN ANCIENT VISION FOR A BRIGHTER FUTURE

We have completed our nutritional exploration of the vegan diet, free of animal flesh and dairy products. We have considered the chemistry and cookery of animal-free foods, and met some of the healthy families who thrive on delicious vegan cuisine. However, the advantages of the vegan diet extend far beyond meeting the R.D.A.'s for protein and calcium. As flesh-eating becomes a practice of the past, we will all enjoy benefits on a global level. Let's consider for a moment the vast and wonderful implications of raising our children on vegan foods, and the kind of world such a diet choice would create.

(Acknowledgment is given here to **Mr. John Robbins**, whose landmark work, **DIET FOR A NEW AMERICA**, available through Gentle World, P.O. Box U, Paia, Maui, HI 96779, provided the data and focus for the following passage upon the scope of effects of the American meat-centered diet. The statements and statistics given are footnoted in his extensive bibliography, and the reader seeking further documentation and inspiration on this vital subject is thus referred to this superb book.)

The medical costs associated with the eating of animal products is staggering, in billions of dollars spent, work days lost, and human suffering endured. These costs would sharply diminish for the simple expedient of evolving the human appetite past that for animal flesh.

The energy costs of **American animal agriculture** is dangerously imbalanced, making it the **most wasteful food production system in the world**. The gas and oil requirements and electrical energy consumption inherent in the raising of beef cattle and dairy products, including the fuel for all the tractors to grow and transport the grain, the water pumps to irrigate the crops and water the millions of animals, and the trucks to transport the cattle and refrigerate the meat products, consumes and wastes more electrical and petroleum energy for calories and usable energy returned, than any other industry on the planet.

American animal agriculture, long hailed as producing inexpensive food, actually **produces the most expensive food on Earth**. The production of meat and dairy products **requires** twenty calories of energy put into the process for every one calorie of usable food energy returned. Growing corn, soybeans and other grains, however, **returns** 60 calories of usable food energy for each one calorie put into the soil.

The supermarket costs of beef and dairy products are kept artificially low through multi-billion dollar government payments to farmers and ranchers, in product price supports, tax benefits, and irrigation subsidies. If beef were sold at the true cost of the process necessary to produce the cellophane wrapped section of cow muscle in the refrigerator case, it would cost an average of between $10.00 and $35.00 per pound. On the other hand, in a box of whole grain cereal, the actual cost of the grain, enough to feed two people a nutritious breakfast for a week, is about six cents, less than the cost of the printed cardboard box in which it is sold.

The energy gluttony, inevitably created by a meat-based diet, makes the food supply of Americans dependent upon a string of oil tankers stretching from our shores to the Persian Gulf, with all the political and economic entanglements that such dependence creates, even leading to threats of war. **A change of American eating habits to a pure vegetarian diet could cut our oil needs substantially, and lessen our dependence on imported oil.**

Ominously, the national meat-eating habit is actually **threatening the very ecosystems of planet Earth** upon which we all depend for our very lives. The tropical rain forests in Central America, South America, and Africa, are vital to the earth's oxygen supply, temperature regulation, and home to millions of unique animal and plant species. Twenty-four hours a day, these vital forests are being leveled by bulldozers to create grazing pastures for beef cattle, large quantities of which are then sold to American meat merchants.

Every hour, three hundred acres of precious forest disappears under the bulldozer blade, an area the size of Pennsylvania every year. The exposed forest floor quickly erodes, producing a desert within a few years of cattle ranching. Forty per cent of the rain forests in Central America that existed in 1950 are now gone. At the current rate of destruction, up to ninety per cent will have disappeared by the end of the next decade.

The tropical rainforests of Central and South America are also the winter homes for our birds, like robins and songbirds that populate the land during the summer and also control insect pests. As the forests disappear, so do the birds. The skies of America are becoming empty and quiet as the bird populations dwindle.

With fewer birds, farmers spray more and more toxic pesticides on crops to kill the now greater number of insects, many of which have become resistant to the most toxic of pesticides. These pesticides, many of which are potent toxins and carcinogens, are sprayed upon our food crops and are building to dangerous levels in all foods. The toxic accumulation is highest in meat and dairy products because the animals that eat pesticide-sprayed feed grains concentrate these poisons in their muscles and fat, so the eater of flesh foods and milk products receives concentrated doses of these toxic chemicals.

Raising animals for food is extremely **wasteful of priceless grain resources.** Animals are notoriously inefficient convertors of food energy to muscle tissue, requiring sixteen pounds of grains and legumes to create one pound of beef. **Ninety per cent of all the grains and legumes grown in the United States are fed to animals. Meanwhile, twenty million people on planet Earth will starve to death this year, for lack of grains and legumes to eat. A child on Earth starves to death every three seconds.**

Yet every year, the beef cattle in America eat ten times the protein and food calories than that consumed by the American people themselves. Just by decreasing their meat consumption by 10%, Americans would create a surplus of 12 million tons of grain each year, enough to eliminate the hunger problem in Africa and America, as well.

Raising animals for food is also by far **the greatest consumer and polluter of fresh water** on the planet today, draining off 60% of all the fresh water used on our continent. Considering the water drawn from the rivers and aquifers, to grow the grain to feed the animals, to water the animals, to clean the manure from the feed lots, and run the slaughterhouse operations, a person eating a **meat-based diet causes 6000 gallons of water to be consumed each day**, just to supply their food, while a person on a **pure vegetarian diet requires just 300 gallons of water each day**. In more graphic terms, the production of each 1000-pound steer consumes enough drinking water to float a naval destroyer.

Fortunately, all these problems, which seem to be dragging us along a collision course to disaster, can be reversed and transformed into forces of rescue, in return for our simple realization that **it is time to change our taste preferences and our food choices**. As American society evolves towards an animal-free diet, wonderful changes will become evident.

The water will become cleaner and more plentiful, the air will become clearer, human suffering from disease and malnutrition will decrease. As this happens, the national financial burden of medical costs and high taxes will diminish, and lending money to help people build new houses, schools, and non-polluting energy sources, like solar and wind energy, will become available. The national debt will decrease, and could be paid off within our lifetime. The erosion of our topsoil, and the poisoning of our life support systems would cease, and a healing of the planet would begin. World hunger could and should disappear.

Farmers and ranchers who now earn their livelihood from animal agriculture can be helped to transition to less costly and destructive forms of food production. With proper planning and financial support, this important evolution could occur with minimal inconvenience to individuals and society. Wisely crafted government programs could supply low interest loans to establish new businesses and purchase equipment, as well as creating programs to help farmers, ranchers, and animal food processors to acquire new agricultural and managerial skills.

It is now time for the citizens of North America, Europe, Australia, and of all countries who follow the fat-laden American style diet, to realize there is something they can do to improve their own fate, on a national level, and in their personal lives and health.

At this time, education is the best hope to produce beneficial changes and salvage our destiny. Many people, especially children and young adults, as well as policy makers, must become aware of the nature and gravity of the situation. As John Robbins declares, "We do not inherit the land from our ancestors, we borrow it from our children."

Besides being a source of nutrition for the body, a vegan style of eating, with its implications for a more balanced ecosystem, cleaner water, feeding of the world's hungry, and a lessening of animal suffering, offers inspiration and guidance to the growing consciousness of children, and the parents responsible for their nurture. Vegan nutrition could also guarantee that there will be a viable planet Earth for our children's children to enjoy.

Children should be educated early as to the importance of kindness and love for animals, and the effects that our food choices have upon the animals and the ecology. This rationale of compassion for, and a connection with all life will make it much easier for children to present and defend their vegan ideals to their peers, as health reasons are not usually prime concerns for energetic children.

WILLOW JAY BASTONE

at 3 months.

The idea of vegan nutrition appears in time-honored texts, in many religions (Judeo/Christian, Genesis 1:29, Daniel, 1:1-40; Hindu - Mahabarata). Perhaps this book is your first encounter with the concept of vegan nutrition. I feel confident that it will not be your last. The philosopher, Goethe, said, "What you know about, you see," and vegan nutrition appears to be an important idea whose time has come.

Now that you know about vegan nutrition, and the principles of balance from which it originates, I predict you will be seeing and hearing more about it, on television, in advertisements, on restaurant menus, and in books and magazines about health. Hopefully, and best of all, you will soon be enjoying vegan cuisine on your own dinner table, and experiencing its benefits in your health, and in the health of those you love.

CONCLUSION

The ancient adage, "As the twig is bent, so grows the tree", is certainly true for the health of our children. The 20th century epidemics of clogged arteries and cancers that plague so many millions of Americans do not suddenly leap upon us from ambush as adults. The artery clogging occurs step by step with each fatty cheeseburger or milkshake consumed, beginning in childhood. The obesity problem gets weightier with each ice cream treat or cheese sandwich eaten. The tendency for cells to cancer increases with each fatty, hormone-laced piece of meat or dairy food consumed.

Although disease is "earned" day by day through dietary transgressions, starting in early childhood, a solid foundation of health can also be established during these formative years. A child can and should grow up with a lean, strong, supple body, with arteries that stay clean and joints that stay flexible through the ninth decade and beyond.

To create a healthy body, ignorance is not bliss. The health-destroying practices of a "fast-food childhood" must be replaced by accurate nutritional information given to children from informed parents and teachers. Using vegan nutrition to nourish the pregnant woman and growing child, as well as creating a satisfying and convenient dietary cuisine, is a major key to a long, healthy life for both parent and child.

This book is witness to the remarkable changes that are occurring in the understanding of human nutrition. Americans are consuming less meat and dairy products, and are benefiting from the changes. The guidelines of balanced vegan nutrition presented here will work for you. If you have special medical conditions, the guidance of a nutritionally knowledgeable health professional is of value. For help in locating such a resource person, consider consulting one of the following organizations:

The American Holistic Medical Association
6932 Little River Turnpike
Annandale, Virginia 22003

VEGEDINE
Society of Vegetarian Dietitians and Nutrition Educators
3835 Route 414
Burdett, NY 14818

The American Vegan Society
501 Old Harding Highway
Malaga, New Jersey 08328

North American Vegetarian Society
P.O. Box 72
Dolgeville, New York 13329

The Earthsave Foundation
706 Frederick St.
Santa Cruz, CA 95062

APPENDIX I

NUTRIENT VALUE OF SELECTED VEGAN FOODS

To illustrate the rich nutrient content found in vegan cuisine, the values for protein, calcium, and iron contained in some popular vegan dishes are given below.

NOTE: The following food ingredients are specially selected for their high content of **protein, calcium, and iron**. Remember, these nutrients abound in **grains**, (and all grain products: breads, pastas, cereals, etc.), **legumes**, (including tofu, lentils, chickpeas, etc.), **dark green, leafy vegetables, nuts**, and **seeds**. The following nutrient values are cited from Handbook of the Nutritional Contents of Foods, the United States Department of Agriculture, Dover Publications, Inc., New York, and Food Values of Portions Commonly Used, C. F. Church, M. D., and Helen Church, B.S., J.B. Lippincott Co.

FOOD & AMOUNT	PROTEIN (grams)	CALCIUM (mgs)	IRON (mgs)
GRAINS:			
Whole Grain Bread (One Slice)	2	50	1
2 medium Baked Potatoes	5	30	2
Millet (4 oz.)	11	23	7
Corn (1/2 cup)	2.2	4	.4
Brown Rice (1 cup)	3.8	18	1
Oats (4 oz.) Raw Flakes (uncooked)	17	170	9
1 bowl Oatmeal	5.4	21	1.7
Cracked Wheat Cereal (2/3 cup)	3	12	1
Barley (1 oz.) dry	2.7	10	1
Bulghur Wheat (1 oz.)	3.1	10	1
Whole Grain Pasta/Spaghetti (1 cup)	8	16	1

FOOD & AMOUNT	PROTEIN (grams)	CALCIUM (mgs.)	IRON (mgs.)
DARK GREEN LEAFY VEGETABLES: (1 cup, cooked)			
Broccoli	5	180	1.6
Kale	5	199	1.6
Chard	3.6	121	3
Collards	5.4	304	1.2
Spinach	5.6	160	4

* Nutrient values calculated with the "Nutrition Wizard" computer program. Public Interest Software, Center for Science in the Public Interest, 1501 16th Street, N.W., Washington, D.C. 20036.

FOOD & AMOUNT	PROTEIN (grams)	CALCIUM (mgs.)	IRON (mgs.)
LEGUMES			
Lima Beans - 1 cup	13	64	5
Most other Beans (i.e., Kidney, Navy, approx. same)			
Broad Beans, 1/2 cup	25	100	7
Snap Beans, green, cooked, 1 cup	2	62	1
Peas - 3/4 cup	20	64	5
Mung Beans, sprouted, 3 1/2 ounces	4	20	1.5
Tofu-1/4 of 1 lb. block	9	150	2
(precipitated w/CaCl 2 - not MgCl 2 - read label)			
Tofu/Grain casserole	13	180	3
(1 cup Tofu; 2 1/2 C. Grain) 1 C. serv.			
Chickpeas, 1/2 cup	21	150	7
Hummus spread (1/2 cup serving)	15	150	4
2/3 cup Garbanzo Beans, 2 tbsp. Tahini			

FOOD & AMOUNT	PROTEIN (grams)	CALCIUM (mgs.)	IRON (mgs.)
NUTS AND SEEDS			
Sesame Butter (Tahini)	9	42	1
2 tablespoons			
WheatGerm - 3 tbsp.	8	20	3
Sunflower Seeds	12	60	3.5
(1/2 cup -1 blender of "Sunny Milk")			
Cashew Nuts (25 nuts)	9	20	2
Peanut Butter (2 tbsp.)	10	15	‹1
Almond & Raisin Mix	20	316	7.5
(1 cup Almonds, 2/3 cup Raisins)			
Dried Apricots, 1/2 cup	5	67	6
Sorghum	0	90	10
(Sweetener for Baked Goods, Granola, etc.)			
Prune Juice - 6 oz.	‹1	25	7.5
"Nutrition Booster Topping" on any Cereal,	20	200	7
in Cookies, etc. 1/4 cup Almonds, 2 tbsp. Wheat Germ, 1/2 cup Raisins			

 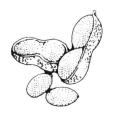 

    Some women find the recommended 74 grams of protein excessive for them, and do not feel their best at such a high protein intake. They will do well to listen to their bodies and adhere more to the more moderate World Health Organization's protein guidelines. They can reduce their intake of concentrated protein foods - tofu, lentils, nut butters, etc. - and increase consumption of complex carbohydrates, like fruits, potatoes, etc. If such subsitutions, are made additional supplemental calcium and iron might be advisable to replace that provided by the lentils, nut butters, etc.

APPENDIX II

PARTIAL NUTRITIONAL ANALYSIS OF POPULAR VEGAN DISHES

Here is a listing of "real meals", free of meat and dairy products, that pregnant women and growing children (as well as the rest of the family!) can enjoy while meeting all their body's nutritional needs.

The suggestions that follow are a mere sampling of the great variety offered by vegan cuisine. Using them as guidelines, with your own imagination and a good vegan cookbook, will help you create a great variety of delicious meals throughout the week. One quickly learns the easy-to-make nutritional favorites.

The recipes for dishes marked with an "*" are found in **THE COOKBOOK FOR PEOPLE WHO LOVE ANIMALS**.

FOOD & AMOUNT	PROTEIN (grams)	CALCIUM (mgs)	IRON (mgs)
BREAKFAST			
1 bowl Whole Grain Cereal (2 oz.)	8	100	2
(Granola* with Almonds & Raisins) and 1 cup Sunflower Milk* or Soy Milk			
Whole Grain Toast (1 slice)	7	70	1.5
with Peanut Butter (1 tbsp)			
6 oz. Scrambled Tofu* (with 2 tbsp. Tahini)	20	210	4
LUNCH			
Garden Green Salad with Tahini Dressing	14	260	5
1 bowl Vegetable Soup* with Beans, Barley, and Carrots	12	220	4
Tofu "Eggless Salad"* sandwich on Whole Grain Bread	20	250	5
(with 4 oz. Tofu Spread, using 2 tbsp. Tahini*, 1 oz. Sprouts, and one sliced Tomato)			
DINNER			
Green Salad with Nutritional Yeast/Tahini Dressing*	14	260	4
Soup - Vegetable/Bean/Grain*, 1 bowl	10	220	4
with 1 slice Whole Grain Bread			
Entree - Vegetable/Grain/Tofu casserole*	16	250	3
- 1 large helping			
Spaghetti with Tomato Sauce	10	35	2
- 1 1/2 cup serving			
Tofu Lasagna* - 1 large helping	16	250	3
Chinese style Vegetables* over Rice	12	200	2
- 1 large helping			
SIDE DISHES			
Steamed Broccoli or Kale,	9	330	6
with Nutritional Yeast Gravy* - 1 serving			
Steamed Carrots* - 1 serving	2	60	‹1
SNACKS AND TREATS			
1 cup Almonds and Raisins	18	316	7.5
mixture eaten during day			
Banana Bread - 2 slices	4	150	2
Protein/Calcium enriched Fruit Smoothie*	15	200	2
using 3 Bananas, 4 oz. Tofu, 2 tbsp. Tahini, 3 cups water			
Fruits of all kinds throughout the day	Vitamin C, minerals, essential fatty acids, amino acids, and fiber.		

APPENDIX III

SIX DAYS OF VEGAN MEALS
FOR PREGNANT WOMEN AND CHILDREN

The following meals are suggested patterns to complete a week of eating in a vegan style, as a complement to the one and two days of menus presented in the main text. The computed nutritional analyses for these meals (available upon request) confirm that vegan nutrition is fully health-supporting for pregnant and lactating women, and growing children.

The meal plans are presented with the assumption that a 32-year-old woman, pregnant with her second child, is preparing each dish/meal for herself, with smaller portions of any of all or the dishes, for her 11-year-old niece, and her 5-year-old son, respectively. Notice the use of foods with "high nutrient density", like peanut butter, fruit bowls, tahini dressings, nut/seed/raisin mixes, and "nice cream" (frozen bananas, peanut butter, and carob), etc. These foods are used to insure that children, who frequently have small stomachs and appetites to match, receive the important energy-containing nutrients they require.

The recipes listed here should provide most essential vitamins and minerals, but a supplement of vitamin B-12 (25 micrograms in divided portions via crushed tablets, drops, etc., during the week) and vitamin D (Maximum 400 I.U. daily if sunlight exposure is inadequate) is recommended. (See "Vitamins" sections in text). Women unsure of the vitamin content of their diet, should employ a prenatal vitamin supplement several times weekly. Supplemental vitamin drops for infants and toddlers administered several times per week is also advised.

Calcium supplements may be used if one attempts to meet the U.S. R.D.A.'s, but, as stated above, these foods easily exceed the calcium requirements set by the World Health Organization and should be entirely adequate for anyone employing the "calcium sparing", moderate-protein, vegan style of eating.

The meal ideas that follow are only suggested patterns; there are many variations upon these themes:

PREGNANT FEMALE, AGE 32 YEARS

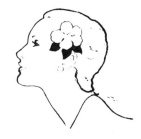

Height 5 ft. 5 in., Weight 139 lbs.
Frame - Medium
Moderately Active

FEMALE, AGE 11 YEARS

Height 4 ft. 7 in., Weight 79 lbs.
Frame - Small
Active

MALE, AGE 5 YEARS

Height 3 ft., 6 in., Weight 40 lbs.
Frame - Small
Active

VEGAN MEAL SUGGESTIONS

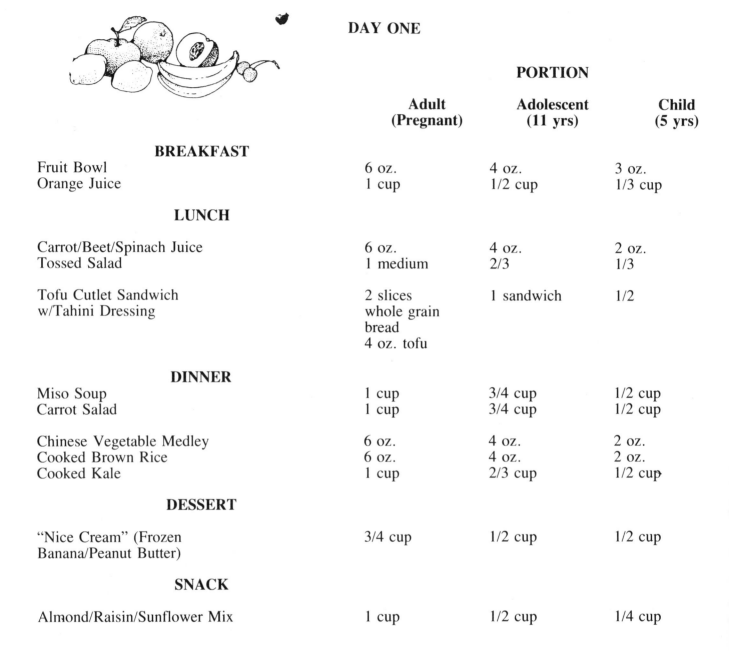

DAY ONE

	Adult (Pregnant)	Adolescent (11 yrs)	Child (5 yrs)
PORTION			
BREAKFAST			
Fruit Bowl	6 oz.	4 oz.	3 oz.
Orange Juice	1 cup	1/2 cup	1/3 cup
LUNCH			
Carrot/Beet/Spinach Juice	6 oz.	4 oz.	2 oz.
Tossed Salad	1 medium	2/3	1/3
Tofu Cutlet Sandwich w/Tahini Dressing	2 slices whole grain bread 4 oz. tofu	1 sandwich	1/2
DINNER			
Miso Soup	1 cup	3/4 cup	1/2 cup
Carrot Salad	1 cup	3/4 cup	1/2 cup
Chinese Vegetable Medley	6 oz.	4 oz.	2 oz.
Cooked Brown Rice	6 oz.	4 oz.	2 oz.
Cooked Kale	1 cup	2/3 cup	1/2 cup
DESSERT			
"Nice Cream" (Frozen Banana/Peanut Butter)	3/4 cup	1/2 cup	1/2 cup
SNACK			
Almond/Raisin/Sunflower Mix	1 cup	1/2 cup	1/4 cup

DAY TWO

	PORTION		
	Adult	**Adolescent**	**Child**

BREAKFAST

Tofu Omelette	4 oz.	3 oz.	2 oz.
Whole Grain Toast	1 slice	1 slice	1/2
w/Peanut Butter	2 Tbsp.	2 Tbsp.	1 Tbsp.
Herbal Tea	1 cup		

LUNCH

Tossed Salad	1 medium	1/2	1/3
w/Tahini/Tamari Dressing	1 ounce	1/2 oz.	1/3 oz.
Mushroom/Barley Soup	6 oz.	4 oz.	2 oz.
Whole Grain Bread	2 slices	1 slice	1 slice

DINNER

Spinach/Mushroom Salad	1 medium	1/2	1/3
Chickpea Loaf	6 oz.	4 oz.	2 oz.
Broiled Zucchini	1/2 large	1/3	1/4

SNACK

Carob Cake	1 slice	1	1/2
Calcium-Fortified Soy Milk	6 oz.	4 oz.	2 oz.

DAY THREE

	Adult	Adolescent	Child
	PORTION		

BREAKFAST

	Adult	Adolescent	Child
Oatmeal	4 oz.	2 oz.	1 oz.
with Sunflower Milk,	2 oz.	1 oz.	3/4 oz.
Raisins and	1/4 cup	1/8 cup	1/8 cup
Slivered Almonds	1/8 cup	1/8 cup	1/8 cup

LUNCH

	Adult	Adolescent	Child
Carrot Salad	1 cup	3/4 cup	1/2 cup
Tofu Eggless Salad	4 oz.	3 oz.	1 oz.
on Rice Cake	1	1	1/2

DINNER

	Adult	Adolescent	Child
Carrot/Beet Juice	6 oz.	4 oz.	2 oz.
Garden Vegetable Soup			
w/Quinoa	6 oz.	4 oz.	2 oz.
Whole Grain Bread	1 slice	1	1/2
Eggplant/Tahini Bake	4 oz.	3 oz.	2 oz.
Steamed Broccoli	4 oz.	3 oz.	2 oz.

DESSERT

	Adult	Adolescent	Child
Oatmeal Cookies	3	2	1
Calcium-Fortified Soy Milk	6 oz.	4 oz.	2 oz.

SNACK

	Adult	Adolescent	Child
Orange Segments	5-10	3-6	2-5
or			
Melon Slices	2-4	1-3	1-2

DAY FOUR

	PORTION		
	Adult	**Adolescent**	**Child**
BREAKFAST			
Buckwheat Pancakes	4 4" cakes	3	2
Maple Syrup	2 Tbsp.	2	1
Calcium-Fortified Soy Milk	6 oz.	4 oz.	2 oz.
LUNCH			
Millet Burger Sandwiches on Whole Grain Bun with "trimmings"	2	1	1/2
Tahini/Tamari Sauce	1 oz.	1/2 oz.	1/4 oz.
Coleslaw	3 oz.	2 oz.	1 oz.
DINNER			
Tomato/Tofu Salad	1 medium	1	1/2
Potato Kugel	4 oz.	3 oz.	2 oz.
String Bean Almondine	3 oz.	2 oz.	1 oz.
DESSERT			
Mixed Fruit Bowl	4 oz.	3 oz.	2 oz.
SNACK			
Peanut Butter	2 Tbsp.	2 Tbsp.	1 Tbsp
and Jelly	1 Tbsp.	1 Tbsp.	2/3 T.
on Whole Grain Bread	1 slice	1	1/2

DAY FIVE

	Adult	Adolescent	Child
		PORTION	
	Adult	**Adolescent**	**Child**

BREAKFAST

	Adult	Adolescent	Child
Whole Grain Wheat/Oats Cereal	4 oz.	3 oz.	2 oz.
with Sunny Milk,	1 cup	3/4 cup	1/2 cup
Raisins,	1/4 cup	1/5 cup	1/5 cup
Chopped Almonds,	1/8 cup	1/8 cup	1/8 cup
and Sliced Peaches	1/4 cup	1/5 cup	1/5 cup

LUNCH

	Adult	Adolescent	Child
Tossed Salad	1 medium	1/2	1/3
Tofu Italian Dressing	1 oz.	1/2 oz.	1/3 oz.
Split Pea/Vegetable Soup	4 oz.	3 oz.	2 oz.
Whole Grain Bread	1 slice	1	1/2 - 1

DINNER

	Adult	Adolescent	Child
Carrot/Beet/Spinach Juice	6 oz.	4 oz.	2 oz.
Carrot Salad	1 cup	1/2 cup	1/3 cup
Corn Tacos with Beans	2 Tacos	1	1/2 - 1
Cooked Broccoli w/gravy	4 oz.		

DESSERT

	Adult	Adolescent	Child
Frozen Fruit Popsicle	1 - 2	1	1/2 - 1

SNACK

	Adult	Adolescent	Child
Almond/Sunny/Raisin Mix	1/2 cup	1/3 cup	1/4 cup
or Orange Juice	4 oz.	3 oz.	2 oz.

DAY SIX

	Adult	PORTION Adolescent	Child
BREAKFAST			
Mixed Fruit Bowl	6 oz.	4 oz.	3 oz.
Orange Juice	1 cup	1/2 cup	1/3 cup
LUNCH			
Spaghetti and Tofu	4 oz.	3 oz.	2 oz.
Steamed Mustard Greens	3 oz.	2 oz.	1 oz.
DINNER			
Tossed Salad	1 medium	1/2	1/3
Vegetable Loaf	4 oz.	3 oz.	2 oz.
Corn on the Cob	2 ears	1 ear	1/2 - 1
Steamed Collards	1 cup	1/2 cup	1/3 cup
DESSERT			
"Nice Cream"	3 oz.	2 oz.	1-2 oz.
SNACK			
Fruit Smoothie	4 oz.	3 oz.	1-2 oz.

DAILY ALLOWANCE	Calories	Protein	Calcium	Iron
Adult Male	2800	65	800	10
Adult Female	2000	55	800	18
Pregnancy	2200	65	1200	18

The following is a six-day analysis of food values
of each daily meal as listed:

	Calories	Protein	Calcium	Iron
Day One	2960	87	974	31
Day Two	2305	95	920	32
Day Three	2357	95	1207	31
Day Four	3751	112	1001	32
Day Five	2748	99	1003	32
Day Six	2626	89	920	32

APPENDIX IV

"ON THE ROAD AGAIN"

(FOOD FOR THE TRAVELING VEGAN)

Any person "on the road" who wishes to eat wisely, safely, and avoid fast food (fat food) restaurants, should travel with a "food satchel" containing the following staple items in plastic containers with well fitting lids. Keep these items on hand:

1. **Nut and Fruit Mix** - any combination of nuts, seeds, raisins, dried fruit, coconut, etc. Handy in airports, on motor trips, etc.

2. **Peanut Butter**

3. **Tahini** - mix with water and tamari to make salad dressing, or to spread on bread.

4. **Tamari** - use on sandwiches, vegetables, like "soy sauce".

5. **Nutritional Yeast -** to mix in salad dressings.

6. **Tofu** - store in sealed container under water - use sliced and seasoned, or mashed as a spread for sandwiches.

7. **Whole Grain Products** - pita "pocket" bread, rice cakes, or whole wheat bread, all are convenient on the road.

   Sandwich ideas- guacamole (avocado), tofu "eggless" salad, peanut butter and banana or fruit spread, etc.

8. **Cereals** - for breakfast - granola, puffed and flaked whole grains, etc. - top with fresh fruit and use soy milk (Edensoy, Ah Soy, bottled nut milks or fruit juice, etc.), instead of dairy milk.

9. **Fresh Drinking Water** - buy it if necessary, and carry it in an insulated bottle with lots of ice - the ice will melt slowly, and the water will stay cold.

10. **Other Beverages** - 100% juice, in small cans, or 3 and 6-pack boxes; seltzer or bottled mineral water.

11. **Fresh Produce** - if you are on an extended trip, some shopping may be necessary to replenish perishables, like lettuce, tomato, sprouts, fruits, tofu, etc.

12. **Necessary Utensils** - silverware, (including cutting knife, and accessories - masher for tofu and/or avocado), plates, bowls, napkins, cutting tray, and travel drinking cups with lids, straws, plastic bags for trash and compost - and don't forget the twist
ties for the plastic bags. For convenience in traveling, keep tahini and tamari in plastic squeeze bottles, and nutritional yeast in a small container with a secure lid.

Handy snacks suitable for car, train or plane:

Bran muffins
Unsalted pretzels
Whole grain bread
Whole wheat bagels
Vegan corn muffins
Whole grain crisp breads
Jams and fruit spreads
Fresh fruits and vegetables
Popcorn

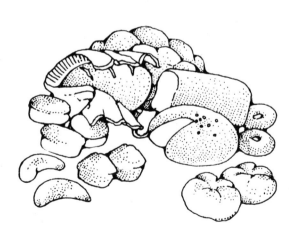

When making airline reservations, be sure to specify your preference for a vegan meal.

If you find yourself at a restaurant, eat from the salad bar, and look for menu items featuring pastas and side dish selections of vegetables. Order soup, an appetizer, and several side dishes. Inform the waiter that you are interested in meatless entrees, and he may know of a special dish that the chef can prepare for such occasions. Advance notice to restaurant staff is both courteous and effective for vegans dining out. Ask how dishes are prepared to make sure non-fat methods are used; i.e., baking, steaming, or broiling. Order sauces on the side.

At the salad bar, choose high-fiber vegetables (broccoli, carrots, kidney beans, spinach, etc.) Beware of cream sauces and other dairy-containing condiments in salad dressings, dessert toppings, as well as high fat condiments; e.g., imitation bacon bits, cheese, etc. When you order a baked potato, avoid butter and keep toppings on the side.

If invited to a friend's house for dinner, give the host as much advance notice as possible of your vegan food preference, and make suggestions for your dinner menu, such as vegetable soup, a large salad, or even a fruit bowl. Most hosts will not feel inconvenienced by such a request, and the awkward scene of refusing a meat entree can be avoided.

APPENDIX V

DAIRY ALTERNATIVES

For those ready to make the big "moooove," here's the way to free yourself from the "dairy connection". At breakfast time, when contemplating what to pour upon your cereal, realize it is quick and easy to make your own non-dairy "milks." The secret is to own a good blender, and use **very** cold water in the recipes. With a little practice, a pitcher of sweet, white, frothy "milk", ready for drinking or pouring on fruit or cereal, can be made in five minutes. Try these one morning soon:

1. <u>For use on your cereal, try this:</u>

Sunny Milk: Start with: 1/2 cup raw sunflower seeds and 1 cup ice cold water. Blend 30-90 seconds until smooth. Fill blender with cold water, and blend to mix. Add sweetener to taste. If sunny milk is prepared the night before, a quick "stir-up" in the blender in the morning will again restore its white, frothy appearance.

Nut Milks: Can be made by adding 1/2 cup nuts; almonds, cashews, etc., or nut butters made of these, instead of sunflower seeds.

Banana Milk: 1/2 blender full of ice cold water. Slice 2 to 3 ripe bananas. Add 1 tablespoon of sorghum, barley malt, maple syrup, or other sweetener. 1/2 teaspoon vanilla. Blend well (30 seconds) and pour on cereal.

Soy Milk: 2 cups cold water, 8 tablespoons soy powder. Blend with vanilla and sweetener to taste.

OTHER BREAKFAST TIME "MILK" BREAKS

1. For a change, try pouring apple juice or other fruit juice on your cereal. It's cold and sweet and takes only a little getting used to. This is especially convenient when traveling.

2. Commercial soy milk preparations (Edensoy, Ah Soy, etc., in the refrigerator case at the health food store) are delicious for drinking (ice cold!), on cereals, etc. Liquid and powdered soy milks are available (Soyagen, Soyamel, etc.), and are fortified with calcium, protein, riboflavin, B-12, and Vitamin D, in levels comparable to those of fortified cow's milk.

(These beverages must not be used as "formula" for feeding infants! There are specially constituted soy-based formulas for this purpose - see "Vegetable Milks for Infants" section).

REPLACEMENTS FOR DAIRY TREATS

TOFU "YOGURT":
(Ice cream substitute)

One 12-ounce cake tofu
Sliced bananas, 1 frozen, 1 fresh
1 teaspoon sorghum or other sweetener
1/4 cup fruit juice or water

This does not have the sour taste of most dairy yogurts.

Blend at medium speed for 45 seconds until creamy. Adding strawberries, cherries, and other fruits will create "fruit-flavored" yogurt. Just before serving, add raisins, sunflower seeds, or fruit of your choice (blueberries, diced peaches, cherries, etc.) Chill in freezer for 30 minutes and serve.

BANANA - TAHINI MALTED: ("Banini")

2 cups water
2 frozen bananas, sliced
1-1/4 tablespoons tahini (sesame seed butter)   Yields 3 cups.
1 teaspoon vanilla.

Combine all ingredients in blender; blend at high speed for one minute, until creamy and smooth. If too thick, add water; if too thin, add more frozen banana.

Tastes like a vanilla thick shake!

For daily drinks, instead of cow's milk, drink clear liquids like water, fruit juices, herb teas, etc. Without dairy fat in your blood you will become leaner and healthier and help reduce your chances of heart attack, clogged arteries, some cancers, and other serious diseases. The only time we should have milk in our diet is when we are infants, nursing at our mother's breast.

VEGETABLE "MILKS" FOR INFANTS

If breastmilk is not available for the nursing infant, the following commercial soy-based formulas are available at supermarkets, health food stores, and pharmacies. They are fortified with vitamins B-12, D, calcium, and other nutrients, and they have been shown to support healthy growth in children. Thus, when breastmilk supplies are limited or need supplementation, the following products are recommended:

1. Soyalac (Loma Linda, California)
2. ProSobee (Mead Johnson, Nutritional Division, Evansville, Indiana)
3. Nursoy (Wyeth Laboratories, Philadelphia, Pennsylvania)
4. Isomil (Ross Laboratories, Columbus, Ohio)

Be sure to follow package directions exactly, and prepare the soy milks with the appropriate volumes of water to assure a healthful concentration of proteins and other nutrients.

The following recipes are for homemade vegetable milks, which can occasionally be substituted for soy milk or breastfeeding. Due to their high protein content, they are not to be used as a steady replacement for breastmilk or properly constituted non-dairy infant formulas.

Recipes for homemade vegetable milks may need straining, depending on baby's age.

Sesame Milk: For 1 quart, soak overnight 6 tablespoons of raw sesame seeds in 1 cup pure water. (Avoid chemicalized city water, especially for babies.) The next morning, drain and rinse seeds, buzz in blender with 2 cups water and 8 pitted dates. Blend until smooth, pour in quart jar, and fill to the top with water. Keep covered in refrigerator, and shake well before each use. It will keep about 2 days. 1/2 teaspoon of nutritional yeast can be added to formula for vitamin B-12, and additional amino acids and minerals.

Vegetable Milk Variations

With one quart water, blend any of the following:

3 Tbsp. sesame butter w/ 3 Tbsp. coconut milk
3 Tbsp. sesame butter w/ 3 Tbsp. sunflower seeds
6 oz. blanched almonds

Sweeten with molasses, maple syrup, or fruits, such as chunks of banana, papaya, apple, peach, etc., as well as dried fruits, like raisins, dates, figs or prunes. A dash of vanilla also adds interest to milks.

1 to 2 Tbsp. soya powder or soya milk can be added to any of the above for increased protein value.

Recipes

Breakfast

SUNNY MILK
Yields 1 quart plus

1 quart water, ice cold
1/2 to 1 cup sunflower seeds
1/2 ripe banana (optional)

1 tablespoon sorghum, or
3 tablespoons raisins

Put all ingredients in blender, and blend at high speed for 2 minutes. Serve as a drink or over granola. Add banana for a thicker milk.
Excellent on breakfast cereal.

VARIATION

Soak seeds overnight, then blend.

TOFU OMELETTE
Serves 1 to 2

1 8-ounce cake tofu
3 tablespoons nutritional yeast
1 tablespoon tamari

2 tablespoons oil
1/4 teaspoon turmeric

Mash the tofu in a bowl. Mix in remaining ingredients. Lightly oil skillet. Place on medium heat. Place batter in skillet and press into omelette shape. Fry until brown on one side, then flip over and brown on other side.

VARIATION

1 onion, diced finely

1/2 sweet red pepper, diced finely

Saute onion and pepper first. Add to batter before frying.

* **Note about sweeteners:** Wherever Sorghum is called for, it can be replaced by Date Sugar, Sucanat, Fructose, Yinny Syrup, Barley Malt or other sweetener of your choice.
  Note about oil: The amount of oil can be halved in all the breakfast recipes.

TOFU YOGURT
Yields 2 cups

1 12-ounce cake tofu
1 banana, frozen and sliced
1 ripe banana, sliced

1-2 tablespoons sweetener
1/4 cup fruit juice or water
1 teaspoon vanilla (optional)

Combine all the ingredients in a blender; blend at medium speed for 45 seconds, until creamy. To serve, add fruit, raisins, and sunflower seeds.

If you use a food processor, you can omit the liquid, then the yogurt will be thicker and creamier.

VARIATION

After yogurt is made, blend with strawberries, blueberries, cherries, peaches, or any fresh fruit. Chill in freezer for 30 minutes.

LIGHT DELICIOUS PANCAKES
Yields approximately 4 dozen

2 cups whole wheat flour, sifted
3 tablespoons maple syrup
1 teaspoon baking soda, sifted
1/3 cup oil
2-1/2 cups tofu milk
  (1-3/4 cups water, blended with
  8-ounce cake of tofu)
  plus
1-1/2 cups water

*Optional:
1/2 cup fresh blueberries
1/4 cup soaked raisins
1/4 cup grated apple
1/4 cup sliced banana

  *You can add ONE of the optional ingredients to the batter.

Mix all dry ingredients together. Mix liquid ingredients and then pour into the dry mixture. Mix thoroughly but leave some lumps which make the pancakes fluffy; if you smooth it out too much, it makes the pancakes tough. You should be able to pour the batter; if too thick, add a little water.

Lightly oil skillet or griddle. Make sure griddle or skillet is very hot (to test, a drop of water should bead on skillet). Pour a tablespoonful of batter on skillet. When it starts to bubble, flip and cook 2 to 3 minutes more. Serve with maple syrup or jam.

LIGHT WHOLE WHEAT BREAD
Yields 2 loaves

2-1/2 cups lukewarm water
1-1/2 tablespoons yeast
1 teaspoon sorghum
3 tablespoons oil

1 teaspoon sea salt
4-1/2 cups whole wheat flour
1-1/2 cups whole wheat pastry flour
2 cups soy flour

In a large bowl, combine the water and yeast. Add the sorghum, oil, and salt. Add 3 cups of the whole wheat flour, 1 cup whole wheat pastry flour, and 1 cup soy flour; blend well. Cover with a cloth and allow to rise for 1 hour.

Add the remaining 1-1/2 cups whole wheat flour, 1/2 cup whole wheat pastry flour, and 1 cup soy flour; mix well. Turn the dough onto a floured board and knead for 10 minutes. Form into 2 loaves. Place in bread pans sprinkled with dried breadcrumbs or cornmeal to prevent sticking. Allow to rise for 1 to 1-1/2 hours.

Preheat oven to 325 F. Bake the loaves for 50 minutes, rotating loaves between the racks after 25 minutes.

Salads

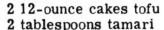

TOFU EGGLESS SALAD
Serves 4

2 12-ounce cakes tofu
2 tablespoons tamari
1 tablespoon oil
2 small onions, diced

2 celery stalks, diced
1/2 teaspoon sea salt
1 teaspoon turmeric
6 tablespoons nutritional yeast

In a medium-size bowl, mash the tofu; add the remaining ingredients and mix well. Refrigerate to keep cold.
Delicious with salad or as a sandwich.

COLD CARROT SALAD
Serves 4 to 6

2 pounds carrots, peeled and sliced
1 large onion, chopped
2 stalks celery, chopped
1/2 cup tahini
1/4 teaspoon basil

5 tablespoons tamari
1-1/2 teaspoons lemon juice
1 teaspoon dill, seed or weed
1/4 teaspoon garlic powder
1/4 teaspoon oregano

Combine the carrots and 4 cups water in a large saucepan; place over medium-high heat and steam for 20 minutes or until soft. Drain off liquid. Transfer the carrots to a large bowl and mash well. Add the remaining ingredients and mix in. Chill and serve cold.

VARIATION

Saute 2 diced onions and 3 diced celery stalks, and add to the carrots.

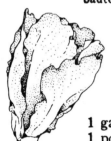

SPINACH MUSHROOM SALAD
Serves 6

1 garlic clove, mashed
1 pound fresh spinach, chopped
1/2 pound fresh mushrooms, sliced
5 tomatoes, cut into chunks

1 head lettuce, shredded
1/4 head cabbage, shredded
2 peppers, sliced
1 garlic clove, diced

Rub large wooden bowl with the mashed garlic. Add all the ingredients except the tomatoes, and toss. Chill for 1 to 2 hours, to allow garlic to permeate the salad.
Serve with oil and vinegar or your favorite dressing. Top with tomatoes.

Dressings

TAHINI DRESSING
Serves 4 to 6

1/2 cup tahini
2/3 cup water
2 tablespoons tamari
1/8 teaspoon garlic powder

1/3 teaspoon paprika
1/8 teaspoon basil
1/8 teaspoon oregano
1/4 small onion, diced

Place all of the ingredients in a blender; blend for 1 minute, until creamy.

TOFU TAHINI DRESSING
Serves 4 to 6

1 cup water
1 8-ounce cake tofu
1/4 cup tahini
1/4 teaspoon caraway seeds
1/4 teaspoon dill weed

1/4 teaspoon garlic powder
2 garlic cloves, diced
2 tablespoons onion, diced
3 tablespoons lime or lemon juice
2 tablespoons tamari

Combine all the ingredients in a blender; blend at high speed for a minute until smooth. Add more liquid (water or stock) if needed. Chill and serve.

BLOND MISO DRESSING
Serves 4

1 cup water
1/4 cup oil
1/8 cup apple cider vinegar
2 tablespoons sorghum
1/4 onion, diced

3 tablespoons blond miso
1 tablespoon nut butter
1/4 teaspoon garlic powder
1/4 teaspoon paprika

Combine all ingredients in a blender; blend at medium speed for a minute until creamy. To make thinner, add more liquid; to make thicker, add more nut butter.

Sauces

MUSHROOM SAUCE
Yields 1 quart

1/2 cup flour
1/2 cup oil
3 cloves garlic, diced
3 onions, diced
1 green pepper, diced
1 stalk celery, diced

1/2 pound mushrooms, sliced
3 cups vegetable stock or water
1/4 cup tamari
1 teaspoon parsley
1 teaspoon garlic powder
1/2 teaspoon sea salt

In a medium sized saucepan, over medium heat, stir in the flour and 1/4 cup of oil. Quick fry until golden brown. Put this mixture aside; using the same saucepan, add the remaining 1/4 cup oil, garlic, onions, celery, and pepper, and saute for 7 minutes. Add the mushrooms and cook 3 minutes more.

Place the stock and the flour mixture in a blender; blend at medium speed for 30 seconds until homogenized. Add blended mixture to saute. Season with tamari, parsley, garlic powder, and sea salt. Cook on low heat for 10 minutes. For a thicker sauce, add more flour.

NUTRITIONAL YEAST GRAVY
Yields 2-1/2 cups

1-1/2 cups stock or water
1/2 cup nutritional yeast
1/4 cup tahini
1/8 onion, diced
1 garlic clove, diced

3 tablespoons tamari
1/2 teaspoon garlic powder
1/2 teaspoon basil
1/2 teaspoon oregano
1/2 teaspoon sea salt

Combine the stock, nutritional yeast and tahini in a blender; blend at medium speed for a minute. Add the remaining ingredients; blend well at high speed. Add more liquid to thin, or tahini to thicken. Season to taste.

Pour gravy into medium sized saucepan; place over low heat and cook until warmed, stirring constantly.

Soups

GARDEN VEGETABLE SOUP A LA GRAIN
Serves 6 to 8

2 tablespoons oil
3 garlic cloves, diced
3 large onions, diced
2 celery stalks, diced
2 carrots, diced
3 potatoes, diced (unpeeled)
2 cups any green vegetable
   (celery tops, cabbage leaves,
   swiss chard, beet greens, etc.)
5 tablespoons tamari

1 cup corn kernels
10 to 12 cups stock or water
1/2 cup any cooked grain
   (rice, kasha, millet, etc.)
1/2 teaspoon dill
1/2 teaspoon basil
1/2 teaspoon sea salt
1/2 teaspoon oregano
1/2 teaspoon garlic powder
1/2 teaspoon parsley

Heat the oil in a large soup pot over medium heat; add the garlic, onions, celery, carrots, and potatoes; saute for 4 minutes. Cut the green leafy vegetables into bite-size pieces, and add to the mixture. Saute for approximately 3 minutes, gradually adding the tamari and corn, until the vegetables are soft. Add the stock, grain, and seasonings. Cook for 2 to 3 hours over low heat.

VARIATION

When soup is done, dilute 5 tablespoons of soy powder in 1 cup of stock; mix into soup to add flavor and thickness.

For a heartier flavor, more protein and nourishment, dilute 3 tablespoons of miso in 1 cup of stock. Add after cooking soup. Never boil miso, as it loses nutrients.

MUSHROOM BARLEY SOUP
Serves 6 to 8

2 tablespoons oil
2 medium onions, diced
2 garlic cloves, diced
2 celery stalks, diced
1 pound fresh mushrooms, chopped
1 cup barley
1/2 cup tamari

1/2 teaspoon garlic powder
1/2 teaspoon sea salt
1 teaspoon parsley, chopped
1 teaspoon dill
10 cups water or stock
2 carrots, diced

In a large soup pot, heat the oil over medium-high heat; add the onions, garlic, celery, and mushrooms, and saute for 4 minutes. Add seasonings, barley, and the water. Reduce heat and simmer for 2 to 3 hours, adding the carrots approximately 45 minutes before soup is finished. To thin soup, add more water.

SPLIT PEA SOUP
Serves 6 to 8

2 cups green split peas
8 cups water or vegetable stock
1 onion, diced
2 celery stalks, diced
2 large carrots, sliced
1 turnip, diced
1 potato, diced
1/3 cup tamari

1/2 teaspoon garlic powder
1 teaspoon sweet basil
1/4 teaspoon sea salt
1/4 teaspoon marjoram
1/8 teaspoon red pepper
2 garlic cloves, diced
2 bay leaves
1/4 cup barley

Combine the peas and the water in a large saucepan; place over medium heat and bring to boil. Reduce heat; add the onion, celery, one carrot, turnip, potato, tamari, and seasonings. Cook for 1 hour, till the peas and all vegetables are soft. Remove the bay leaves.

Transfer mixture to a blender, and blend at high speed for 1 minute, until well mixed. This will take 3 to 4 blenders full. Add 1 clove of diced garlic while blending.

Pour back into pot. Add the barley, the remaining carrot and the bay leaves; season to taste. Cook over low heat for 2 hours, stirring often.

MISO SOUP
Serves 4 to 6

2 tablespoons oil
4 garlic cloves, diced
2 large onions, diced
2 carrots, cut into large pieces
2 celery stalks, diced
7 cups vegetable stock
1 cup small lima beans
1/4 teaspoon oregano

1/4 teaspoon garlic powder
1/4 teaspoon sea salt
1/4 teaspoon parsley
1/8 teaspoon paprika
2 tablespoons tamari
1 cup whole wheat or
    spinach noodles (optional)
4 to 6 tablespoons of miso paste

In a soup pot, heat the oil over medium-high heat; add the garlic, onions, carrots, and celery; saute for 7 minutes till golden brown. Add the stock, beans, and spices; cook for 1 to 2 hours over medium-low heat. Add the noodles, and cook until tender.

Dilute the miso paste in 1 cup of warm stock; add to the soup, and simmer for 30 minutes.

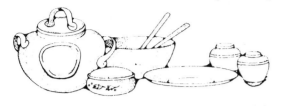

Main Dishes

CHINESE MEDLEY
Serves 6 to 8

4 tablespoons oil
5 garlic cloves, diced
5 large onions, cut into chunks
4 stalks celery, cut into chunks
3 peppers, sliced
1/2 head cabbage, shredded
1/3 cup tamari

1/4 teaspoon ginger powder
1/8 teaspoon red pepper
1/4 teaspoon sea salt
1/2 teaspoon garlic powder
3 tablespoons arrowroot powder
1 cup mung bean sprouts

Heat the oil in a wok or skillet over high heat, until very hot; add 2 cloves of the garlic and all the onions. Saute for 5 minutes, stirring often.

Add the celery, peppers, and half of the spices; cook for 3 or 4 minutes. Add the cabbage and the remaining spices except for the garlic. Sift the arrowroot through a strainer or sifter, and sprinkle into the vegetables, stirring constantly.

Cook for 5 minutes, till the mixture thickens; then add the remaining garlic and the sprouts. Reduce heat, cover and simmer for 3 or 4 minutes before serving.

MILLET BURGERS
Yields 3 dozen

3 cups millet
3 tablespoons oil
5 garlic cloves, diced
6 large onions, diced
3 stalks celery, diced
3 carrots, diced
1/3 cup tamari

1 teaspoon basil
1 teaspoon parsley
1 teaspoon garlic powder
1 teaspoon sea salt
1/2 teaspoon paprika
3 tablespoons peanut butter or tahini
1/2 cup wheat germ or bran

Bring 6 cups of water to a boil in a large pot; add the millet and cook over medium-low heat for 20 to 25 minutes, or until soft.

Heat the oil in a skillet over medium heat; add the garlic and onions, and saute for 3 minutes, until the onions are golden. Add the celery and carrots; cook for 4 minutes, until all the vegetables are tender.

Add the seasonings: 2 tablespoons tamari, 1/2 teaspoon each of parsley, basil, garlic powder, and sea salt; stir constantly. Remove from heat.

Preheat oven to 350 F. Oil cookie sheet. In a large bowl, combine the millet and the sauteed vegetables. Add the peanut butter, remaining tamari and remaining seasonings. Add wheat germ or bran to bind the mixture, and to reach a consistency that holds together.

Form the mixture into patties and place them on the cookie sheet. Bake for 15 minutes; turn over and bake for 15 minutes more, checking them periodically to prevent burning.

Great served in sandwiches.

POTATO KUGEL
Serves 6

10 potatoes, grated
1 large onion, diced
1/2 cup soy powder
3 tablespoons tamari
1/2 teaspoon garlic powder

1/2 teaspoon paprika
1/2 teaspoon basil
1/2 teaspoon sea salt
Dash of red pepper

Preheat oven to 350 F. Discard any potato water that has accumulated while grating.

In a large bowl, combine the potatoes, onion, soy powder, and spices. If too moist, add 1/3 cup bran, flour, or more soy powder. Oil an 8" x 12" casserole dish; put potato mixture in it. Bake for approximately 1 hour, checking it periodically. It should get golden brown on the top.

TOFU CUTLETS
Serves 4

2 8-ounce cakes tofu
2 tablespoons tamari
1 cup nutritional yeast
1/2 teaspoon oil

1/4 teaspoon basil
1/4 teaspoon oregano
1 large onion, diced
2 cloves garlic, diced

Drain tofu well of its water. Cut tofu into slices 1/4" thick. Saute onions and garlic until golden brown. Make a mixture of tamari, oil, saute, and spices. Add other favorite spices if you like.

Place tofu pieces in mixture and let marinate, then dip into nutritional yeast until thoroughly covered.

Oil a cookie sheet. Place tofu pieces on sheet and bake at 325 F. for 5 to 7 minutes on each side, then broil until crispy. This dish can also be cooked in a frying pan with a little oil. Easy and delicious.

VARIATION

Add 2 tablespoons of lemon juice to marinate mixture.

EGGPLANT TAHINI BAKE
Serves 6 to 8

2 tablespoons oil
6 large onions, sliced
1/4 cup tamari
1/2 teaspoon garlic powder
1/4 teaspoon paprika
1/4 teaspoon parsley

1/4 teaspoon basil
1/4 teaspoon oregano
3 garlic cloves, diced
1 cup tahini
2-1/2 cups water
4 eggplants, peeled and sliced thin

Heat the oil in a large frying pan over medium-high heat. Add the onions, 2 tablespoons of the tamari, the seasonings, and the diced garlic.

In a medium sized bowl, combine the tahini, remaining tamari, and water; mix well, until creamy and not watery. Add seasonings, if desired. Preheat oven to 350 F.

In two 8" x 12" baking dishes, pour a thin layer of tahini sauce, to prevent sticking; add a layer of eggplant, and a thin layer of sauteed onions. Cover with tahini sauce, and repeat layering. Sprinkle paprika on top of last layer of sauce. Bake for 45 minutes, until eggplant is tender (test with a fork).

Delicious served cold in a sandwich.

Treats

BANANA ICE CREAM

1 ripe banana per bowl

Peel and freeze the banana. Put the frozen banana through a Champion Juicer set up to homogenize, or through any appliance that homogenizes.

OATMEAL COOKIES
Yields 5 dozen

3/4 cup oil
1 cup date sugar
3/4 cup sorghum
1/3 cup soymilk
2 teaspoons vanilla
2-1/2 cups flour

1/2 teaspoon baking soda
1 teaspoon sea salt
3 cups rolled oats
1/2 cup raisins
3/4 teaspoon cinnamon

Add oil, sweetener, soy milk, and vanilla together, and beat until smooth. Add remaining ingredients and mix well.

Bake at 350 F. for about 10 minutes, or until the undersides just start turning brown.

CAROB CAKE
Yields 2 8-inch round cakes

1/2 cup oil or margarine
1/2 cup date sugar
1/2 cup sorghum
4 tablespoons soy powder
   and 6 tablespoons water
1/2 cup carob powder
   and 1/2 cup water

1-1/2 teaspoons vanilla
3 cups whole wheat pastry flour
1 teaspoon baking soda
1 teaspoon Postum
1/2 cup mixed nuts
   and raisins, chopped
3/4 cup thick nut milk (see recipe)

Preheat oven to 350 F. Oil two 8'' baking pans. In a large bowl, combine the oil, date sugar, and sorghum; mix together the soy powder and 6 tablespoons water, and add this to the mixture.

Combine the carob and 1/2 cup of water; add to the mixture. Add vanilla. In a separate bowl, combine the flour, soda, Postum, and nuts and raisins; add to the liquid mixture. Mix in the thick nut milk.

Divide the batter equally between the pans; bake for 30 to 35 minutes, testing by sticking a toothpick in the center of cake—if it comes out dry, the cake is done.

VARIATION

For vanilla cake, omit the carob, and add 3 teaspoons more vanilla and 1/2 cup more flour.

APPENDIX VII

RECOMMENDED READING

VEGAN NUTRITION: PURE AND SIMPLE
Michael A. Klaper, M.D.
Gentle World
P.O. Box U
Paia, Maui, HI 96779

THE MOST NOBLE DIET
George Eisman, R.D.
3835 Route 414
Burdett, NY 14818

THE VEGETARIAN SOURCEBOOK
Keith Akers
Vegetarian Press
P.O. Box 10248
Arlington, VA 22210

PROBLEMS WITH MEAT
John A. Scharffenberg, M.D.
Woodbridge Press Publishing Co.
Santa Barbara, CA 93111

THE ANIMAL CONNECTION
Agatha Thrash, M.D. and
Calvin Thrash, M.D.
Yucchi Pines Institute
Seale, AL 36875

DIET FOR A NEW AMERICA
By John Robbins
$13.95
Available through, Gentle World, Inc.
P.O. Box U
Paia, Maui, HI 96779

DON'T DRINK YOUR MILK!
Frank A. Oski, M.D.
Mollica Press, Ltd.
1914 Teall Ave.
Syracuse, NY 13206

THE COOKBOOK FOR PEOPLE WHO LOVE ANIMALS
Gentle World
P.O. Box U
Paia, Maui, HI 96779
$9.95 postpaid.

PERIODICALS OF INTEREST

Vegetarian Times
P.O. Box 570
Oark Park, Illinois 60303

Ahimsa
The American Vegan Society
501 Old Harding Highway
Malaga, New Jersey 08328

Vegetarian Voice
c/o North American Vegetarian Society
P.O. Box 72
Dolgeville, New York 13329

Vegetarian Journal
c/o Baltimore Vegetarians
P.O. Box 1463
Baltimore, Maryland 21203

ACKNOWLEDGMENTS

The author gratefully acknowledges the valuable suggestions made by friends and colleagues in the "vegetarian nutritional network" in the production of this work:

Deep appreciation is expressed to Light and Sun and to the pioneering members of Gentle World, Inc., the vegan educational organization, formerly of Umatilla, Florida, now on Maui, where so much practical experience and insight into the vegan diet was and is gained.

Special thanks is expressed to Jay and Freya Dinshah, of the American Vegan Society, for their encouragement and assistance in the production of this work. Jay's vision and energy have been an indespensible guiding force in the nurturing of vegan ideas and ideals in the United States. Freya's experience as a vegan mother and leadership as vegan educator, especially in the field of childraising and nutritional education, has been invaluable. The author appreciates Freya's generosity in granting permission to share some of her excellent recipes and ideas here.

Nutrition professionals like John MacDougall, M.D., Kailua, Hawaii; Agatha Thrash, M.D., Seale, Alabama; George Eisman, R.D., Watkins Glen, NY; Hanoch Talmor, M.D., Gainesville, Florida; Neal Barnard, M.D., Washington, D.C.; Ronald Hoffman, M.D., N.Y.; and Steven Tiger, P.A., Monroe, N.Y.; provided guidance in sections on vitamins, protein, and other vital nutrients. Bob Leroy's (New York) reflections on calcium contents of vegan foods was especially appreciated as was Keith Akers' inspiring **Vegetarian Sourcebook.**

The guidance from parents who have raised or are raising vegan children, like John and Arlyn Phoenix, Florida; Victoria Moran, Kansas City; Marcia Pearson and husband, Kent McCormack, Bothell, Washington; Pat Bastone, Sydney, British Columbia, Canada; and James and Barbara Peden, Wayden Lake, Idaho; contained the "Voice of experience", and increased the practical value of this booklet.

The author acknowleges the La Leche League's permission to use their excellent Information Sheet - No. 105, "Baby's First Solid Food," as a source of valuable ideas for feeding babies.

Helpful ideas for infant feeding were found in "Feeding Your Baby Vegetarian", by Margaret Nofziger, nutritionist for "The Farm."

The editorial and legal guidance of friend and colleague, Andrew Fields, Esq., is greatly appreciated. Special thanks to Jeanie Greenbaum for her helpful suggestions and many hours at the word processor, and to Cynthia Klaper for her insightful editing contributions and loving support.

A FOOTNOTE ON PHOTOGRAPHS

The vegan approach to life includes far more than nutrition. It extends to living gently upon the planet, minimizing the pain and suffering inflicted upon all sentient beings. Thus, not only does the ethical vegan person refrain from eating animal flesh and dairy products, but also from using consumer goods, like leather, wool, silk, tallow soaps, etc., derived from animals.

Current photographic and printing techniques employ gelatin to hold the light-sensitive emulsion upon the celluloid film. Gelatin, of course, is made from the hooves, horns, and skins of cows and other slaughtered creatures. Consequently, most people who are vegan for ethical reasons, avoid utilizing standard photography, as the heart of its process, the film, is derived from the exploitation of animals.

The photographs reproduced in this book are included to provide inspiring visual examples of vegan families, and thereby increase enthusiasm for vegan nutrition. As people obtain their nutrition without eating flesh and milk products, the lives of millions of innocent animals will be spared. Thus, photographs have been utilized in this book with the feeling that the animals would give their permission, in the interest of creating a gentler, healthier planet.

An encouraging note - As photographic technology advances, the process is becoming more "electronic", utilizing video tape style technology. Innovators in the photographic and printing industries predict that in the near future, gelatin-containing photographic film will be replaced by completely vegan materials and techniques. All vegan people, and the animals, look forward to that day.

REFERENCES

1. (a) McGill, H. Persistent problems in the pathogenesis of atherosclerosis. Arteriosclerosis 4:443, 1984.

   (b) Editorial: The progression of atherosclerosis. Lancet 1:791, 1985.

   (c) Flynn, M. Serum lipids in humans fed diets containing beef or fish and poultry. Am J. Clin Nutr 334:2734, 1981.

   (d) Flynn, M. Dietary "meats" and serum lipids. Am J. Clin Nutr 35:935, 1982

   (e) O'Brien, B. Human plasma lipid responses to red meat, poultry, fish, and eggs. Am J Clin Nutr 33:2573, 1980.

   (f) Fehily, a. The effect of fatty fish on plasma lipid and lipoprotein concentrations. Am J. Clin Nutr 38:349, 1983.

   (g) Kromhout, D. The inverse relation between fish consumption and 20-year mortality from coronary heart disease. N Engl J Med 312:1205, 1985.

   (h) Gordon, T. Diabetes, blood lipids, and the role of obesity in coronary heart disease risk in women. The Framingham study. Ann Intern Med 87:393, 1977.

2. "Chemical Contaminants in Breast Milk", New England Journal of Medicine, 3/26/81, p. 792.

3. Current Pediatric Diagnosis & Treatment, 7th Edition, by C. Henry Kempe, M.D., et al, Lang Medical Publications, 1982, p. 772.

4. Ferrer, J. Milk of dairy cows frequently contains a leukemogenic virus. Science 213:1014, 1981.

5. (a) Holman, R. The natural history of atherosclerosis. The early aortic lesions as seen in New Orleans in the middle of the 20th century. Am J Pathol 34:209, 1985.

   (b) Enos W. Pathogenesis of coronary disease in American soldiers killed in Korea. JAMA 158:912, 1955.

   (c) Smoak, C. G., et al. Relation of obesity to clustering of cardiovascular disease risk factors in children and young adults. The Bogalusa Heart Study. Am J Epidemiol. 1987 Mar. 125(3). P 364-72.

6. Awadalla, S.G. et.al. "Pregnancy complicated by intraamniotic infection by Salmonella typhi." Obstet-Gynecol. 1985 Mar. 65 (3 Suppl.) P 30S-31S.

7. Kempe, H., op.cit. p. 772.

8. Listeria meningitis, Kempe, H., op.cit. p. 787.

8a. (a) Falandysz, J. Organochlorine pesticides and polychlorinated biphenyls in herring from the southern Baltic, 1983. Z-Lebensm-Unters-Forsch. 1986 Feb. 182(2). P 3131-5.

   (b) Eisenberg, M., et al. Organochlorine residues in finfish from Maryland waters 1976-1980. Journal of Environmental Science and Health 'B]. 1985 Dec. 20(6). P 729-42.

8b. Linsalata, P., et al. Comparative pathway analysis of radiocesium in the Hudson River Estuary: environmental measurements and regulatory dose assessment models. Health-Physics. 1986 Sep. 51(3). P 295-312.

Footnotes 73 through 76 are now listed as References 8a - 8d.
Footnotes 77 through 80 are now listed as References 11a - 11d.

8c. (a) Jana, S., et al. Heavy metal pollutant induced changes in some biochemical parameters in the freshwater fish Clarias batrachus L. Acta-Physiologica-Hungarica, 1986. 68(1), P 39-43.

(b) Skogheim, O.K., et al. Mortality of smolt of Atlantic salmon, Salmo salar L., at low levels of aluminum in acidic softwater. Bulletin of Environmental Contamination and Toxicology. 1986, Aug. 37(2). P 258-65.

(c) Shukla, N.P., et al, Effect of heavy metals on fish--a review. Review of Environmental Health. 1985. 5(1) P 87-99.

(d) Galindo, L., et al. Correlations between lead, cadmium, copper, zinc, and iron concentrations in frozen tuna fish. Bulletin of Environmental Contamination and Toxicology. 1986 Apr. 36(4). P 595-9.

8d. Czarnezki, J.M., Accumulation of lead in fish from Missouri streams inpacted by lead mining. Bulletin of Environmental Contamination and Toxicology. 1985 May. 34(5). P 736-45.

9. Mercury poisoning, Harrison's Principles of Internal Medicine, Edition, McGraw-Hill Co., N.Y., 1974, p. 670, 1970.

10. (a) Mercury-induced blindness in children; Goodman, L.S., and Gilman, A. eds.: The Pharmacological Basis of Pharmacology, Toxicology and Therapeutics for Physicians and Medical Students (4th ed.; New York; Macmillan Co., 1970).

(b) Arena, J.M. Poisoning: Chemistry, Symptoms, Treatments (Springfield, Ill.:Charles C. Thomas, Publisher, 1963).

11. Mental retardation in children, Kempe, H., op.cit., p. 627.

11a. (a) McKeown-Eyssen, G.E., et al. Methyl mercury exposure in northern Quebec. I. Neurologic findings in adults. American Journal of Epidemiology. 1983 Oct. 118(4). P 461-9.

(b) Valciukas, J.A., et al. Neurobehavioral assessment of Mohawk Indians for subclinical indications of methyl mercury neurotoxicity. Archives of Environmental Health. 1986 Jul-Aug. 41(4). P 269-72.

(c) Lommel, A., et al. Organochlorines and mercury in blood of a fish-eating population at the River Elbe in Schleswig-Holstein, FRG. Archives of Toxicology 'Suppl]. 1985. 8. P 264-8.

(d) Jensen, A.A., et al. Polychlorinated terphenyls (PCTs) use, levels and biological effects. Science of Total Environment. 1983 April. 27(2-3). P 231-50.

(e) Mykkanen, H., et al. Dietary intakes of mercury, lead, cadmium and arsenic by Finnish children. Human Nutrition/ Applied Nutrition. 1986 Feb. 40(1). P 32-9.

11b. (a) The New England Journal of Medicine, March 26, 1981, P 792.

(b) Noren, K. Levels of organochlorine contaminants in human milk in relation to the dietary habits of the mothers. Acta-Paediatrica-Scandinavia. 1983 Nov. 72(6). P 811-6.

(c) Siddiqui, M.K., et al. Placenta and milk as excretory routes of lipophilic pesticides in women. Human Toxicology. 1985 May. 4(3). P 249-54.

11c. "Fish and Fish Oil are 'Second Line' Therapies," The McDougall Newsletter, Nov/Dec 1986.

11d. "What about fish oil's risks?" Letter to the Washington Post "Health" section by C. Wayne Callaway, October 14, 1986.

12. Hepatitis in children, Kempe, H., op. cit., p. 478.

13. Hydrocarbons in meat, Modern Meat, Orville Schell, Random House, New York, p. 156-166, 1984.

14. (a) Falandysz, J. Organochlorine pesticides and polychlorinated biphenyls in herring from the southern Baltic, 1983. Z-Lebensm-Unters-Forsch. 1986 Feb. 182(2). P 3131-5.

(b) Eisenberg, M., et al. Organochlorine residues in finfish from Maryland waters 1976-1980. Journal of Environmental Science and Health 'B]. 1985 Dec. 20(6). P 729-42.

15. Hydrocarbons in dairy products: results of inquiry into contamination of animal feed by polychlorinated biphenyls. State of Michigan, Department of Public Health, published 1967-1970.

16. (a) Schell, O., op.cit., p. 156-166.

(b) Thrash, A., M. D., The Animal Connection, published Yuchi Pines Institute, Seale, AL, 1980.

17. (a) Schwartz, et al. Physicians' Handbook on Pesticides, San Diego: California Public Interest Research Group and the Department of Community Medicine, University of California, San Diego Medical Center, 1980.

(b) Harrison's Principles of Internal Medicine, Seventh Edition, P. 1683-85, 1974.

18. (a) Noren, K. Levels of organochlorine contaminants in human milk in relation to the dietary habits of the mothers. Acta-Paediatr-Scand. 1983 Nov. 72(6). P. 811-6.

(b) Siddiqui, M.K., and Saxena, M.C., "Placenta and Milk as Excretory Routes of Lipophilic Peticides in Women", Human Toxicology, 1985, May, 4(3), P. 249-54.

19. Schell, O., Op.cit., p. 279-302.

20. (a) Aristimuno, G.G., et al. Influence of persistent obesity in children on cardiovascular risk factors: the Bogalusa Heart Study. Circulation. 1984 May. 69(5). P 895-904.

(b) Arntzenius, A.C., "Diet, Lipoproteins, and the Progression of Coronary Atherosclerosis", Drugs, 1986, 31 Suppl 1, P. 61-5.

21. (a) Akman, D., et al. Heart disease in a total population of children: the Bogalusa Heart Study. South-Med-J. 1982 Oct. 75(10). P 1177-81.

(b) Berenson, G.S., et al. Cardiovascular risk factors in children. Should they concern the pediatrician? Am-J-Dis-Child, 1982 Sep. 136(9). P 855-62.

22. (a) Phillips, R.L.: Role of lifestyle and dietary habits in risk of cancer among Seventh Day Adventists. Cancer Res. 35:3513-3522, 1975 (supplement).

(b) Phillips, R.L., et al. Coronary heart disease mortality among Seventh Day Adventists with differing dietary habits: a preliminary report. Am J Clin Nutr 31:S191-198, 1978.

23. Kahn, R.H., et al. Association between reported diet and all cause mortality: twenty-one year follow up on 27,530 adult Seventh Day Adventists. Am J Epidemiology, 119:775-787, 1984.

24. Normal Pregnancy in Vegan Women

(a) Thomas, J., et al. Proceedings of the Nutritional Society, 36, 46a., 1977.

(b) Sanders, T. A. B. (1977). The Composition of Red Cell Lipid and Adipose Tissue in Vegans, Vegetarians, and Omnivores. PHD Thesis: University of London.

Normal Growth in Vegan Children

(c) Dwyer, J.T., et al. (1978): Preschoolers on Alternate Lifestyle Diets. Journal of American Dietetic Association, 72, 264-270.

(d) Fulton, J. R., et al (1980): Preschool Vegetarian Children. J. Am. Diet. Ass'n. 76, 361-365.

(e) Sanders, T.A.B. (1981): An anthropometric and dietary assessment of the nutritional status of vegan preschool children. Journal of Human Nutrition. 35, 349-357.

25. Journal of the American Dietetic Association 77:61-60, 1980.

26. (a) J. Stamler, "Population Studies," in Nutrition, Lipids, and Coronary Heart Disease (New York: Raven Press, 1979) ed. R.I. Levy, et al.

(b) Beilin, L.J., "Vegetarian Approach to Hypertension", Canadian Journal of Physiology and Pharmacology, June, 1986, 64(6), P. 852-5.

27. (a) Burke, G.L., et al. Cardiovascular risk factors and their modification in children. Cardiol-Clin. 1986 Feb. 4(1). P 33-46 (Review).

(b) Sanders, T.A., et. al., "Blood Pressure, Plasma Renin Activity and Aldosterone Concentations in Vegans and Omnivore Controls", Human Nutrition, 1987, June, 41 (3), P. 204-11.

(c) Fisher, M., et. al., "The effect of Vegetarian Diets on Plasma Lipid and Platelet Levels", Archives of Internal Medicine, June, 1986, 146(6), P. 1193-7.

28. K. K. Carroll and H. T. Khor, Progress in Biochemical Pharmacology 10: 308, 1975. Cited in B.S. Reddy, et al: "Nutrition and Its Relationship to Cancer," Advances in Cancer Research 32:237, 1980.

29. (a) Badenoch, A.G. (1952) Brit.Med.J. 2, 668.

(b) J. A. Halstead, et al. "Serum Vitamin B-12 Concentration in Dietary Deficiency," The American Journal of Clinical Nutrition 8: 374, 1960.

(c) M.C.Higginbottom, et al, "A Syndrome of Methylmalonic Aciduria, Homocystinuria, Megaloblastic Anemia and Neurologic Abnormalities in a Vitamin B-12 Deficient Breast-fed Infant of a Strict Vegetarian," New England Journal of Medicine 299 (7): 317, 1978.

30. (a) Badenoch, A.G.J. (1954) R. Soc. Med. 47,426.

(b) F. R. Ellis, et al, "Veganism, Clinical Findings and Investigations," The American Journal of Clinical Nutrition 23(3): 249, March 1970.

31. Ellis, Frey R. and V.M.E. Montegriffo, The Health of Vegans, Plant Foods and Human Nutrition. Vol. 2, pp. 93-103, 1971. Pergamon Press, Northern Ireland.

32. Sanders, T.A.B., Vegetarianism: Dietetic and Medical Aspects, Journal of Plant Foods (1983)5, 3-14.

33. (a) Sanders, T.A.B., et.al. Haematological studies on vegans. British Journal of Nutrition (1978) 40, 9. P. 14.

(b) Carter, J.P., et.al., "Preeclampsia in Reproductive Performance in a Community of Vegans", Southern Medical Journal, 1987, June 80(6), P. 692-7.

34. Sanders, op.cit. Ref. 24 (e). British Journal of Nutrition.

35. Journal of the American Dietetic Association. 77:61-69, 1980.

36. (a) J. Stamler, "Population Studies," in Nutrition, Lipids, and Coronary Heart Disease (New York: Raven Press (1979) ed. R. I. Levy, et al.

(b) Snowdon, D.A., et. al., "Meat Consumption and Fatal Ischemic Heart Disease", Preventive Medicine, 1984, Sept. 13(5), P. 490-500.

37. McGill, H., Op.cit.

38. (a) Sweeney, J. Dietary factor that influence the dextrose tolerance test: a preliminary study. Arch.Intern.Med. 40:818, 1927.

(b) Snowdon, D.A., et. al., "Does a Vegetarian Diet Reduce the Occurance of Diabetes?", American Journal of Public Health, 1985, May 75(5), P. 507-12.

39. McMahon, B. Urine oestrogen profiles of Asian and North American women. Int. J. Cancer 14:161, 1974.

40. MacDonald, P. Effect of obesity on conversion of plasma androstenedione to estrone in postmenopausal women with and without endometrial cancer. Am. J. Obstet. Gynecol. 130:448, 1978.

41. (a) Solomon, L. Rheumatic disorders in the South African Negro. Part I. Rheumatoid arthritis and ankylosing spondylitis. South African Medical Journal 49:1292, 1975.

  (b) Parke, A. Rheumatoid arthritis and food: a case study. British Medical Journal 282(6281):2027-9, June 20, 1981.

42. (a) Lucas, P. Dietary fat aggravates active rheumatoid arthritis. Clin. Res. 29:754A, 1981.

  (b) Stroud, R. Comprehensive environmental control and its effect on rheumatoid arthritis. Clin Res. 28:791A, 1980.

  (c) Parke, A. Rheumatoid arthritis and food: a case study. Br. Med. J. 282:2027, 1981.

43. Korenblat, P. Immune responses of human adults after oral and parenteral exposure to bovine serum albumin. J. Allergy 41:226, 1968.

44. Baker, M. D., Sidney M., Gesell Institute of Human Development Update, Volume 3, No. 2, 1984.

45. Op.cit., Sanders (Ref. 24f) p. 14

46. Ibid, P. 14

47. Stamler, J., Op.cit.

48. Statistics from Dept. of Consumer Affairs, U. S. Dept. of Agriculture. 1985.

49. Bar, R. Fluctuations in the affinity and concentration of insulin receptors on circulating monocytes of obese patients: effects of starvation, refeeding and dieting. J Clin Invest 58:1123, 1976.

50. (a) Sims, E. Obesity and hypertension. Mechanisms and implications for management. Special communications. JAMA 247:49, 1982.

  (b) Margetts, B.M., et. al., "Vegetarian Diet in mild Hypertension: a Ramdomised Controlled Trial", British Medical Journal Clinical Research Edition, 1986, Dec. 6, 293(6560), P. 1468-71.

51. Benson, M. D., Current Obstetric & Gynecologic Diagnosis & Treatment, 4th Edition, Lange Medical Publications, P. 399. 1982.

52. Ibid, P. 458.

53. Eisman, R.D., G. L., The Most Noble Diet, Diet-Ethics, Miami Beach, FL. 1984.

54. Akers, K., Vegetarian Sourcebook, Vegetarian Press, P. O. Box 10238, Arlington, Virginia 22210, Pages 24

54. (a) Brenner, B. Dietary protein intake and the progressive nature of kidney disease: The role of hemodynamically mediated glomerular injury in the pathogenesis of progressive glomerular sclerosis in aging, renal ablation and intrinsic renal disease. N. Engl. J. Med. 307:652, 1982.

  (b) Wiseman, M.J., et. al., "Dietary Conposition and Renal Function in Healthy Subjects", Nephron, 1987, 46(1), P. 37-42.

55. (a) Hegsted, M. Urinary calcium and calcium balance in young men as affected by level of protein and phosphorus intake. J. Nutr. 111:553, 1981.

  (b) Linkswiler, H. Calcium retention of young adult males as affected by level of protein and of calcium intake. Trans. NY Acad. Sci. 36:333, 1974.

56. World Health Organization, Recommended Daily Allowances -1984, Division of Nutrition, United Nations Plaza, New York.

56a. Carter, J.P., et al. Preeclampsia and Reproductive Performance in a Community of Vegans. South-Med-J. 1987 Jun. 80(6). P 692-7.

57. Akers, op. cit., P. 2-29.

58. Ibid, P. 29-33.

59. (a) For corn: C. Kles, et al, "Determination of First Limiting Nitrogenous Factor in Corn Protein for Nitrogen Retention in Human Adults". The Journal of Nutrition 86:350, August 1965.

(b) For wheat: S. B. Vaghefi, et al, "Lysine Supplementation of Wheat Proteins," The American Journal of Clinical Nutrition 27:1231, 1974.

(c) J. Lee, et al, "Nitrogen Retention of Young Men Fed Rice with or without supplementary chicken," The American Journal of Clinical Nutrition 24: 318, 1971.

(d) P. Markakis, "The Nutritive Quality of Potato Protein", in Protein Nutritional Quality of Foods and Feeds, pt. 2, ed. m. Friedman (New York: M. Dekker, 1975).

(e) E. Kofranyi, F. Jekat, and J. Muller-Wecker, "The Minimum Protein Requirement of Humans Tested with Mixtures of Whole Egg Plus Potato and Maize Plus Beans," Hoppe-Seyler's Zeitschrift for Physiologische Chemie 351(12): 1485, 1970.

60. Amino Acid Content of Food and Biological Data on Protein, Food, and Agriculture Organization of the United Nations. Rome, 1970.

61. Krupp & Chatton, Current Medical Diagnosis & Treatment, Lange Medical Publications, P. 782-783, 1982.

62. B. C. Parker, "Rain as a source of vitamin B-12," Nature 219:617, 10 August, 1968.

63. A. M. and C. L. Thrash, Nutrition for Vegetarians (Seale, Alabama: Thrash Publications, 1982) P. 68.

64. Ellis, M.D., F. R., et al, Veganism, Clinical Findings and Investigations, The American Journal of Clinical Nutrition, Vol. 23, No. 3, March 1976, P. 249-255.

65. Anonymous, "Contribution of the Microflora of the Small Intestine to the Vitamin B-12 Nutriture of Man," Nutrition Reviews 38(8):274, August, 1980.

65 (a). 1. A. M. and C. L. Thrash, Nutrition for Vegetarians (Seale, Alabama: Thrash Publications, 1982), p.

66. Ellis, op. cit., P. 250.

67. Crane, et al. Vitamin B-12 Status of Vegans. Weimar Institute. 1986.

68. Eisman, George, Journal of North American Vegetarian Society, Volume 12, No. 4, 1985.

69. New England Journal of Medicine, March 26, 1981, P. 792.

70. Baker, op. cit. Gesell Institute.

71. Lewinnek, G. The significance and a comparative analysis of the epidemiology of hip fractures. Clin Ortho Related Res 152:35, 1980.

72. Mazess, R. Bone mineral content of North Alaskan Eskimos. Am J. Clin Nutr. 27:916, 1974.

73. (a) Falandysz, J. Organochlorine pesticides and polychlorinated biphenyls in herring from the southern Baltic, 1983. Z-Lebensm-Unters-Forsch. 1986 Feb. 182(2). P 3131-5.

(b) Eisenberg,M., et al. Organochlorine residues in finfish from Maryland waters 1976-1980. Journal of Environmental Science and Health †B]. 1985 Dec. 20(6). P 729-42.

74. (a) Jana, S., et al. Heavy metal pollutant induced changes in some biochemical parameters in the freshwater fish Clarias batrachus L. Acta-Physiologica-Hungarica, 1986. 68(1), P 39-43.

(b) Skogheim, O.K., et al. Mortality of smolt of Atlantic salmon, Salmo salar L., at low levels of aluminum in acidic softwater. Bulletin of Environmental Contamination and Toxicology. 1986, Aug. 37(2). P 258-65.

(c) Shukla, N.P., et al, Effect of heavy metals on fish--a review. Review of Environmental Health. 1985. 5(1) P 87-99.

(d) Galindo, L., et al. Correlations between lead, cadmium, copper, zinc, and iron concentrations in frozen tuna fish. Bulletin of Environmental Contamination and Toxicology. 1986 Apr. 36(4). P 595-9.

75. Czarnezki, J.M., Accumulation of lead in fish from Missouri streams inpacted by lead mining. Bulletin of Environmental Contamination and Toxicology. 1985 May. 34(5). P 736-45.

76. Linsalata, P., et al. Comparative pathway analysis of radiocesium in the Hudson River Estuary: environmental measurements and regulatory dose assessment models. Health-Physics. 1986 Sep. 51(3). P 295-312.

77. (a) McKeown-Eyssen, G.E., et al. Methyl mercury exposure in northern Quebec. I. Neurologic findings in adults. American Journal of Epidemiology. 1983 Oct. 118(4). P 461-9.

(b) Valciukas, J.A., et al. Neurobehavioral assessment of Mohawk Indians for subclinical indications of methyl mercury neurotoxicity. Archives of Environmental Health. 1986 Jul-Aug. 41(4). P 269-72.

(c) Lommel, A., et al. Organochlorines and mercury in blood of a fish-eating population at the River Elbe in Schleswig-Holstein, FRG. Archives of Toxicology 'Suppl]. 1985. 8. P 264-8.

(d) Jensen, A.A., et al. Polychlorinated terphenyls (PCTs) use, levels and biological effects. Science of Total Environment. 1983 April. 27(2-3). P 231-50.

(e) Mykkanen, H., et al. Dietary intakes of mercury, lead, cadmium and arsenic by Finnish children. Human Nutrition/ Applied Nutrition. 1986 Feb. 40(1). P 32-9.

78. (a) The New England Journal of Medicine, March 26, 1981, P 792.

(b) Noren, K. Levels of organochlorine contaminants in human milk in relation to the dietary habits of the mothers. Acta-Paediatrica-Scandinavia. 1983 Nov. 72(6). P 811-6.

(c) Siddiqui, M.K., et al. Placenta and milk as excretory routes of lipophilic pesticides in women. Human Toxicology. 1985 May. 4(3). P 249-54.

79. "Fish and Fish Oil are 'Second Line' Therapies," The McDougall Newsletter, Nov/Dec 1986.

80. "What about fish oil's risks?" Letter to the Washington Post "Health" section by C. Wayne Callaway, October 14, 1986.

81. (a) Lewinnek, G. The significance and a comparative analysis of the epidemiology of hip fractures. Clinical Orthopedics and Related Research 152:35, 1980.

(b) Parfitt,A. Dietary risk factors for age-related bone loss and fractures. "Lancet" 2:1181, 1983.

82. Roberts, H. Potential toxicity due to dolomite and bonemeal. Southern Medical Journal 76:556, 1983.

83. (a) Paterson, C. Calcium requirements in man: a critical review. Postgrad Med J 54:244, 1978.

(b) Heaney,R. Calcium nutrition and bone health in the elderly. Am J Clin Nutr 36:986, 1982.

84. (a) Oski, M.D., Frank, Don't Drink Your Milk!, Mollica Press, Ltd., Syracuse, N.Y., 1983, pp. 24-27.

(b) A. D. Narins, in A. Bezkorovainy. Biochemistry of Nonheme Iron (New York: Plenum, 1980). P. 47-126.

85. Krupp, M.D., M.A., Current Medical Diagnosis & Treatment, 1982, Lange Medical Publications, P. 972.

86. White, P. I., ed., et al, Let's Talk About Food (Acton, Massachusetts: Publishing Sciences Group, 1974), p. 211.

87. Kempe, op. cit., P. 883.

88. Benson, op. cit., P. 627.

89. Ibid, P. 809.

90. New England Journal of Medicine, op. cit.

91. Journal of the American Dietetic Association 77:61-19, 1980.

92. Schell, op. cit. 279

93. Akman, M. op.cit.

94. (a) Holman, R. The natural history of atherosclerosis. The early aortic lesions as seen in New Orleans in the middle of the 20th century. Am. J. Pathol 34:209, 1958.

(b) Scott M. Grundy, M.D., et al, Rationale of the Diet - Heart Statement of the American Heart Association - Report of Nutrition Committee, Circulation 65, No. 4, 1982.

95. Ibid.

96. (a) Hill, P. Environmental factors and breast and prostatic cancer. Cancer Res 41:3817, 1981.

(b) Stanley, T. Cancer of the prostate: An analysis of some important contributions and dilemmas. Monographs in Urology, 1982.

97. (a) Y. Nishizuka, "Biological Influence of Fat Intake on Mammary Cancer and Mammary Tissue: Experimental Correlates," Preventive Medicine 7(2): 218, June, 1978.

(b) P. Hill, et al, "Diet and Prolactin Release," The Lancet 2: 806, 9 October 1976.

(c) P. Hill, et al, "Diet and Endocrine-Related Cancer," Cancer 39: 1820, 1977.

(d) MacMahon, B. Urine oestrogen profiles of Asian and North American women. Int. J. Cancer 14:161, 1974.

98. Scharffenberg, M.D., M.P.H., Director Community Health Education, San Joaquin Community Hospital, Personal Communication. 1980.

99. (a) Staszewski, J. Age at menarche and breast cancer. J. Natl Cancer Inst 47:935, 1971.

(b) Kagawa, Y. Impact of Westernization on the nutrition of Japanese: Changes in physique, cancer, longevity and centenarians. Prev. Med. 7:205, 1978.

(c) Rosen, P. Breast carcinoma in women 35 years of age or younger. Annals of Surgery, 199:133, 1984.

100. Saenz de Rodriguez, C. Environmental Hormone contamination in Puerto Rico. N. Engl. J. Medicine, 310:1741, 1984.

101. Schell, op.cit.

102. Sanders, Ellis, op.cit.

103. (a) When a Child Has Repeated Colds Think of Milk Allergy. Consultant, January, 1968, p. 41.

(b) Milk Has Something for Everybody? Journal of the American Medical Association 232(5) 539, May 5, 1975.

(c) Recurrent Abdominal Pain in Children: Lactose and Sucrose Intolerance, A Prospective Study. Pediatrics 64:43-45, July, 1979.

104. Korenblat, P. Immune responses of human adults after oral and parenteral exposure to bovine serum albumin. Journal of Allergy. 41:226, 1968.

105. Ibid.

106. (a) Unrecognized Disorders Frequently Occurring Among Infants and Children from the Ill Effects of Milk. Southern Medical Journal 31:1016, September, 1938.

(b) Add Milk to Your GI Suspect List. Patient Care, February 15, 1976, p. 116-126.

107. Lindahl, O., Vegan regimen with reduced medication in the treatment of bronchial asthma. Journal of Asthma, 1985, 22(1): 45-55.

108. Parke, A.L., Rheumatoid Arthritis and Food: A Case Study. British Medical Journal (Clin Res) 1981. June 20;282 (6281): 2027-9.

109. Op. Cit. See Ref. 105.

110. Schell, op. cit.

111. Regenstein, L. How to Survive in America the Poisoned, Acropolis Books, 1982, p. 103.

112. (a) The Case Against Heated Milk Protein. Atherosclerosis 13: 137-139, January-February, 1971.

(b) Further Evidence in the Case Against Heated Milk Protein. Atherosclerosis 15:129, January-February, 1972.

(c) Milk Protein and Other Food Antigens in Atheroma and Coronary Heart Disease. American Heart Journal 81:189, February, 1971.

(d) Clifford, et al. Homogenized bovine milk xanthine oxidase: a critique of the hypothesis relating to plasmalogen depletion and cardiovascular disease. American Journal of Clinical Nutrition 38, August 1983, P 327-332.

(e) Sacks, F.M., "Plasma Lipoprotein Levels in Vegetarians", Journal of the American Medical Association, 1985, Sept. 13, 254(10), P. 1337-41.

113. Burke, et al. Cardiovascular risk factors and their modification in children. Cardiol-Clin. 1986 Feb. 4(1). P 33-46. (Review).

114. (a) Carroll, K. K. Op. cit.

(b) Gray, G., et al. Diet and hormone profiles in teenage girls in four countries at different risk for breast cancer. Cancer Prev. Med. 11:108-113, 1982.

115. Ferrer, J. Milk of dairy cows frequently contains a leukemogenic virus. Science 213:1014, 1981.

116. Ibid: 1015.

117. A Multiple Share of Myeloma. Medical World News. May 16, 1969, P. 23.

118. Thrash, A. Op. cit., Chapter 5.

118a. (i) A Multiple Share of Myeloma. Medical World News, May 16, 1969, P. 23.
(ii) What Causes Cancer on the Farm? Medical World News, January 14, 1972, P. 39.

119. Snowden, M.D., Published findings, Department of Epidemiology, Loma Linda University, California. 1980.

120. (a) Phillips, R.L., et al. Mortality among California Seventh Day Adventists for selected cancer sites. JNCI 65:1097-1107, 1980.

(b) Dwyer, J.T. 1983 Nutrition status and alternative lifestyle diets with special reference to vegetarianism in the USA, P 343-410 in Reichaig, M. CRC Handbook of Nutritional Supplements Volume 1; Human Use. Boca Raton, Florida. CRC Press, 1983.

(c) Keys, A. Aravanis, C., et al. The diet and all causes death rate in the Seven Countries Study. Lancet 2:58-61, 1981.

(d) Ellis, F.R., et al. The Health of Vegans. Plant Foods in Human Nutrition., Vol 2, P. 93-103, 197, Pergamon Press, Northern Ireland.

121. Ellis, Op. cit.

122. (a) Smith, A.D.M., "Veganism, A Clinical Survey with Observations of Vitamin B-12 Metabolism". The British Medical Journal 1: 1655, 16 June, 1962.

(b) Parker, B.C. "Rain as a source of vitamin B-12". Nature 219: 617, 10 August, 1968.

(c) Ellis, F.R., et al. "Veganism, Clinical Findings and Investigations". The American Journal of Clinical Nutrition 23(3): 249, March 1970.

123. (a) International Nutritional Anemia Consultative Group. The Effects of Cereals and Legumes on Iron Availability. Nutrition Foundation, Washington, 1982.

(b) Allen, L.H., Calcium bioavailability and absorption: a review, American Journal of Clinical Nutrition, 35: April, 1982. pp. 783-808.

124. (a) Nnakwe, N., et al. Calcium and phosphorus utilization by omnivores and lacto-ovo vegetarians fed laboratory controlled lactovegetarian diets. Nut. Reports International 331:1009-1014, 1985.

(b) "Calcium Bioavailability". Contemporary Nutrition, Volume 11, No. 8, 1986.

125. Honey and botulism. Kempe, op. cit., P. 622.

126. (a) Bahna, S. L., and Heiner, D. C.: Allergies to Milk. New York, Grune and Stratton, 1980.

(b) Gerrard, J. W., Mackenzie, J.W.A., Goluboff, N., et al: Cow's Milk Allergy; Prevalence and Manifestations in an Unselected Series of Newborns. Acta Paediatr Scand, Supplement 234, 1973.

(c) Gryboski, J.D.: Gastrointestinal Milk Allergy in Infants. Pediatrics 40:354, 1967.

NOTES:

Gentle Products

The Cookbook for People Who Love Animals

No Meat • No Eggs • No Dairy
No Sugar or Honey
No Cholesterol • High in Fiber

$9⁹⁵

Over 350 totally vegetarian (vegan) recipes, written by the producers and caterers of the annual Celebrity Vegetarian Banquet.

"A COOKBOOK WHOSE TIME HAS FINALLY COME."
Helen Nearing

Pregnancy, Children and the Vegan Diet

by Michael Klaper, M.D.

$9⁹⁵

A practical "how-to-do it" guide to creating good health without the use of animal products during pregnancy, lactation and in growing children.

**A READING MUST FOR ALL PARENTS
& PARENTS TO BE**

Diet for a New America

by John Robbins
Pulitzer Prize Nominee

$13⁹⁵

Stillpoint Publishing

Diet for a New America is a monumental work, revealing the effects that dietary choices have upon the very survival of our planet.

"A MASTERFULLY WRITTEN EXPOSE"

Vegan Nutrition: Pure and Simple

by Michael Klaper, M.D.

$9⁹⁵

Vegan Nutrition: Pure and Simple is a medical doctor's prescription for personal and planetary health.

JUST WHAT THE DOCTOR ORDERED!

Help Yourself to Health

by Michael Klaper, M.D.

Audio Cassette
Tape Series
Length: 30 min.

Price per tape: **$7⁰⁰**

Gentle World is a tax-exempt charitable organization. Your contributions over and above book and material orders help us to reach out to many more potential supporters of animal rights.

For further information, please write:
Gentle World • P.O. Box U • Paia, Maui, HI 96779

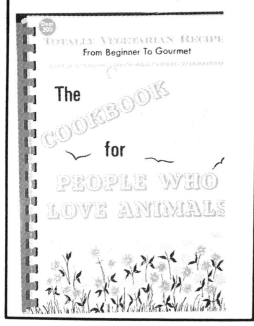

Vegan Nutrition: Pure and Simple
by Michael Klaper, M.D.

 # VN01   **Price: $9.95**

INQUIRE FOR RESALE PRICES

* Vegan Meal Plans and Recipes

* Thoroughly documented facts that will inspire you to improve your eating habits.

NEW REVISED EDITION

VEGAN NUTRITION: PURE AND SIMPLE is a medical doctor's prescription for personal and planetary health. Within its pages, Michael Klaper, M.D., discusses and scientifically documents all aspects of vegan nutrition as the foundation of a healthier life.

Just What the Doctor Ordered *!*

This easy to read evolutionary book

Includes -

* the perils of eating meat, fish, chicken, dairy products and eggs.

* answers to **all** your vegan nutrition questions, such as:

How to get your protein, calcium and vitamin B-12, **without** consuming animal products.

Vegan Nutrition: Pure and Simple

replaces the "Basic Four" with the "Vegan Six" food groups.

1. WHOLE GRAINS and POTATOES	4. NUTS and SEEDS
2. LEGUMES	5. FRUITS
3. GREEN and YELLOW VEGETABLES	6. VITAMIN and MINERAL FOODS

All the nutritional requirements for human health that were just presented can be conveniently (and safely) met by consuming ample portions each day from the "food families" of the "Vegan Six" Food Groups that follow. **"Balance"** in the vegan diet, that is, sufficient amounts of all the essential nutrients, is achieved by eating an appropriate number of servings from **each** group of the "Vegan Six" each day.